Leon Litwack has contributed articles to the *New England Quarterly, Midway Magazine,* and the *Journal of Negro History.* His book *North of Slavery: The Negro in the Free States, 1789-1860* was published in 1961. At present, Professor Litwack is with the Department of History at the University of Wisconsin.

THE AMERICAN
LABOR MOVEMENT

THE AMERICAN
LABOR MOVEMENT

By Leon Litwack

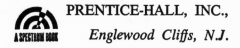

PRENTICE-HALL, INC.,
Englewood Cliffs, N.J.

Current printing (last digit):
13

© 1962 by Prentice-Hall, Inc., *Englewood Cliffs, N.J.*

Library of Congress Catalog Card No.: 62-13726

Printed in the United States of America

02406-C

For my Son and Daughter

John Michael

and

Ann Katherine

Table of Contents

INTRODUCTION   1

I. BACKGROUND OF DISCONTENT   3

THE MACHINE   4

Shoemakers (1864), *4*
A Shoe Worker (1899), *5*
A Currier (1879), *8*
A Printer (1899), *9*

LOSS OF STATUS   10

A Machinist (1883), *10*

CONDITIONS OF LABOR   15

Robert D. Layton (1883), *15*

THE COMPANY STORE   17

A Massachusetts Quarryman (1879), *17*
Samuel Gompers (1899), *18*

THE COMPANY TOWN   18

Pullman Strikers (1894), *18*
U.S. Strike Commission on Pullman Rents
(1895), *20*

ABSENTEE OWNERSHIP   21

John R. Lawson (1915), *22*

II. ORGANIZATION   26

WHY ORGANIZE?   28

Cigar Makers' International Union of America
(1864), *28*
Samuel B. Donnelly (1899), *30*

John A. O'Connell (1914), *31*
John Mitchell (1914), *32*

WHY STRIKE?   34

Samuel Gompers (1899), *34*

THE AMERICAN FEDERATION OF LABOR: "PURE AND
SIMPLE" UNIONISM   36

Adolph Strasser (1883), *36*
G. W. Perkins (1899), *37*
The A.F. of L. and the Socialists: Samuel Gompers v. Morris Hillquit (1914), *37*

THE INDUSTRIAL WORKERS OF THE WORLD: REVOLU-
TIONARY UNIONISM   42

Preamble of the I.W.W. (1908), *42*
William D. Haywood (1915), *43*
Joe Hill: I.W.W. Songwriter (1882-1915), *46*

THE CONGRESS OF INDUSTRIAL ORGANIZATIONS: INDUS-
TRIAL UNIONISM   49

Minority Report of Resolutions Committee on Organization Policies: A.F. of L. Convention (1935), *49*

III. RESPONSES TO UNIONISM   52

THE THREAT OF ALIEN IDEOLOGIES   53

The Nation (1877), *53*
Rev. Henry Ward Beecher (1877), *56*

CONTENTMENT OF THE WORKING CLASS   58

A Massachusetts Mill Owner (1883), *58*
A New Hampshire Mill Manager (1883), *59*

THE PREROGATIVE AND RESPONSIBILITY OF THE EM-
PLOYER   64

Thomas H. Wickes (1894), *64*
George F. Baer (1902), *66*
Marcus A. Hanna (1902), *67*

LABOR RACKETEERING   68

  Charles Piez (1914), *69*
  Subcommittee on Labor Unions of the Committee
    on Legislation, City Club of New York (1937),
    71

UNIONISM AND PERSONAL LIBERTY: ARE THEY COM-
  PATIBLE?   74

  Dudley Taylor (1914), *74*
  Clarence S. Darrow (1915), *75*
  Finley Peter Dunne (1920), *77*
  Walter P. Reuther v. Senator Barry Goldwater
    (1953), *78*

IV. THE WEAPONS OF RESISTANCE   82

THE "YELLOW-DOG" CONTRACT   83

  Western Union Telegraph Co. (1883), *83*
  Hitchman Coal & Coke Co. v. Mitchell (1917),
    84

THE BLACKLIST   85

  Iron Founders' and Machine Builders' Association
    of the Falls of the Ohio (1863), *85*
  A Telegraph Operator (1883), *86*

THE INJUNCTION   87

  U.S. Industrial Commission (1902), *87*
  Eugene V. Debs (1894), *88*

THE COMPANY UNION   90

  John L. Lewis (1934), *90*

FINKS, OPS, HOOKERS, AND THE HOOKED   92

  Glossary (1938), *92*
  Soliciting Work (1917 and 1920), *94*
  The Professional Strikebreaker (1936), *95*
  Labor Espionage, Inc. (1936), *100*
  A Hooker (1936), *107*

THE ARSENAL OF RESISTANCE   108
    Lake Erie Chemical Co. (1936), *108*

V. ORGANIZING THE UNORGANIZED: THE 1930's   113

    "Talking Union" (1941), *113*

THE LEGAL BASIS   115
    Norris-LaGuardia Act (1932), *115*
    National Industrial Recovery Act (1933), *116*
    National Labor Relations (Wagner) Act (1935),
    116

INDUSTRIAL WAR: *Fortune* Magazine (1937)   117

BIG STEEL, LITTLE STEEL: RECOGNITION AND CONFLICT   133
    Manifesto: American Iron and Steel Institute
    (1936), *133*
    "It Happened in Steel" (1937), *134*
    "Little Steel" (1937), *146*
    National Labor Relations Board (1938), *151*

VI. LABOR AT MIDCENTURY: MEMORIES AND
    REALITIES   153
    "The Haunted Hall: I.W.W. at Fifty"—Dan
    Wakefield (1955), *154*
    "What Really Ails the Unions" (1959), *160*
    "Organizing the Unorganized" (1955), *163*
    "The Myth of the Happy Worker"—Harvey
    Swados (1957), *169*

Introduction

Organized labor is an acknowledged force in American society. It is legal, respectable, often powerful, and increasingly businesslike. Significant changes have altered its traditional role as a besieged "underdog." The modern trade union leader is more of an administrator than an agitator, often the head of a vast business empire with branches scattered throughout the country; he takes his seat at the conference table as an equal of the representative of management. Although the strike is still resorted to on occasion (the picket line less so), most of the work is done at the conference table. "Thirty years ago," a union official remarked in 1958, "the important thing was for a union leader to know how to organize economic strength. Organize. Strike. Settle. That was labor-management relations. But today, with laws and labor boards, almost all of our problems are settled at the conference table through negotiations. This requires new skills, a different kind of intelligence. Now, it is diplomacy instead of the big stick."

Compared to his predecessors, the modern trade unionist is better treated on the job, receives higher wages, works a shorter day and week, obtains more "fringe" benefits, is better protected against accidents and illness, and generally enjoys a higher standard of living. He maintains his union membership without fear of employer reprisal. While the union has thus given him a greater feeling of security, it has not, however, been able to immunize him from seasonal layoffs, business dislocations, technological unemployment, installment buying, and climbing prices—nor has it materially lessened the monotony and drudgery of much of factory labor.

Nevertheless, the economic gains of the American worker, particularly in the post-World War II era, have been impressive. Such progress has tended, in fact, to obscure a history punctuated with strife, suspicion, and human misery. Few of labor's gains came easily; many of them had to be won at a considerable cost of lives and property. What helped to make possible the comparatively high standards of mid-twentieth century labor were generations of workers organized into trade unions and willing to employ the only effective weapon in their possession: the ability to stop production. And more often than not, this had to be accomplished in a hostile atmosphere. To the modern trade unionist, however, as to the ordinary citizen, the names of Homestead, Pullman, Cripple Creek, Ludlow, and Lawrence evoke few responses. Likewise, the names of early union leaders are all but forgotten. "The labor agitator of the early days," Eugene Debs once observed, "held no office, had no title, drew no salary, saw no footlights, heard no applause, never saw his name in print and fills an unknown grave."

This book of readings does not pretend to be a comprehensive history of the American labor movement; such accounts are readily available elsewhere, as are more specialized studies of the machinery of collective bargaining, wage determination, labor legislation, and trade union structure. Instead, these readings are directed toward a better understanding of the heritage of organized American labor—the conditions which prompted its rise and frequent eruptions, the men, principles, and tactics that guided (or misled) it, and the ideology and weapons employed to check, frustrate, or destroy its effectiveness. To underscore the progress that has been made and the obstacles which first had to be surmounted, much of the material is drawn from the crucial decades of the late nineteenth and early twentieth century and the 1930's. Such an emphasis may be of more than academic value, for the ability of the labor movement to meet successfully the new challenges of organization, automation, corruption, and apathy may well depend on the extent to which it is able to recapture some of the impetus and dedication that gave it birth.

I. Background of Discontent

Although industrialization was well under way by 1860, its full implications were not apparent until after the Civil War. Statistics document the rapid transformation of the American economy in the postwar years: the augmented railroad systems crisscrossing the country, the increased output of iron and steel, the accelerated exploitation of natural resources, the multiplication of capital investments in industry, and the steady movement of foreign immigrants, Southern Negroes, and farmers (or their sons and daughters) into the cities and manufacturing centers. But indices of industrial growth cannot measure the full impact of industrialization, the ways in which it revolutionized American society, politics, religion, and industry, or the significant effect it had on the tastes and standards of postwar generations. And statistics of production can only suggest the impact of industrial change on the producers: the laboring class.

Just as industrialization drastically altered the processes of production, so it wrought significant changes in the American class structure. Class lines assumed a new and foreboding rigidity. Although outlets remained through which the more enterprising, fortunate, or ruthless could still achieve economic power and escape working-class status, the number of Horatio Alger rags-to-riches stories declined perceptibly—in fact if not in fiction. More and more workers resigned themselves to permanent working-class status, discarding old notions of independence and illusions about the nobility of labor, for escape had become too costly and there was little that was noble about labor in the mechanized industries of the late nineteenth and twentieth centuries. The machines made obsolete many of the skilled trades of the ante bellum years, drawing the once self-respecting and independent handicraftsmen into the drudgery and monotony of factory life, where they were called upon to perform only one step in the minutely divided and automatic processes of mass production.

And, yet, industrialization unquestionably elevated the United States to a world power, produced ever greater quantities of consumer goods for both domestic and world consumption, and substantially increased

3

the standard of living of millions of Americans. Publicists and most politicians hailed the material blessings of the mechanized civilization, as did a substantial number of clergymen and university presidents. But generations of Americans paid a heavy price for industrial progress and failed to share its blessings. Perhaps these were the necessary victims of the industrial process, who might have contented themselves with the realization that they were helping to build a greater civilization. Unfortunately, such realizations could not pay bills, feed mouths, or clothe bodies. And these, more than the glories of the new civilization, were increasingly uppermost in the minds of millions of American laborers. Protest they did, but workers found that they possessed little bargaining power as individuals; industrial freedom, a much heralded term, consisted of the right to work at conditions arbitrarily prescribed by the employer or not to work at all. And that was the way of starvation.

The following selections, drawn from contemporary investigations of conditions of labor, illustrate some of the ways in which industrial change affected the lives of American workers.

THE MACHINE

Shoemakers (1864) *

Comparatively few people are aware of the quiet, steady revolution that is going on in the business of shoemaking, and particularly as that business is conducted in Lynn. Previous to the introduction of the original sewing machines, which are now universally used for the binding and stitching of the uppers, but little or no improvement or even change had been made in the manufacture of shoes. The awl, the bristle and thread, the lapstone and hammer, with plenty of "elbow grease" were, as they had been for years, the main appliances of the shoemakers, and little was known or thought of laborsaving machinery. After a time, women's nimble fingers were found inadequate to the demand, and sewing machines soon transformed the old-fashioned "shoe-binder" into a new and more expensive class of "machine girls" whose capacity for labor was only limited by the capabilities of the machines over which they presided. Iron and steel came to the aid of wearied fingers and weakened eyes. This was the beginning of the new era, which is destined to produce results big with lasting benefits to our flourishing city.

It is scarcely ten years since the first introduction of machinery of any kind into the manufacture of shoes in this city. Everything was done by

* From *Fincher's Trades' Review*, March 26, 1864.

hand, even to the cutting out of the soles, which was a slow process, and required the expenditure of a large amount of physical force. The introduction of sole-cutting and stripping machines, although used sparingly, was the first indication that a change was to take place in the business of shoemaking; but no one, even ten years ago, would have dared to prophesy that the change was to be so immediate and so great. The rapid progress that has been made during that time, and *especially within the past year or two,* in the introduction of machinery in shoemaking, has been beyond all previous calculation. It may almost be said that handwork has already become the exception, and machinery the rule. The little shoemaker's shop and the shoemaker's bench are passing rapidly away, soon to be known no more among us; and the immense factory, with its laboring steam engine and its busy hum of whirling wheels, is rising up in their place to change the whole face of things in this ancient and honored metropolis of the "workers in the gentle craft of leather."

The problem as to how best to bring in and concentrate the vast army of men and women employed in the shoe manufacture of Lynn is one that has attracted the attention of many thinking minds among our businessmen, but it has never been satisfactorily solved until now. Machinery, and particularly the sewing machine, has done in a few short months what years of theorizing and speculation could not do. It has demonstrated that the factory system can be successfully and profitably introduced into the shoe business; in fact, that, with the rapid strides which the business has made within a few years, it is the only system that can be made available for its successful application in the future. Of course, the new system is yet in its infancy—the business is yet in a transition state; but the wheels of revolution are moving rapidly, and they never move backward. Operatives are pouring in as fast as room can be made for them; buildings for "shoe factories" are going up in every direction; the hum of machinery is heard on every hand; old things are passing away, and all things are becoming new.

A Shoe Worker (1899) *

Q. What is the present condition of your trade now in reference to work and wages?

* From the testimony of Horace M. Eaton, General Secretary-Treasurer of the Boot and Shoe Workers' Union, September 21, 1899. U.S. Congress, House, *Report of the Industrial Commission on the Relations and Conditions of Capital and Labor Employed in Manufactures and General Business,* 56th Cong., 2d Sess., House Doc. 495 (Washington: U.S. Government Printing Office, 1901), VII, 359, 361, 363.

A. As to work, very good; as to wages, poor.

Q. How much less than they have been?

A. Well, that would be a difficult question to answer, more or less based upon opinion. I might go back in my own experience as a workman at the bench. Eleven years ago I used to be able to earn myself, lasting shoes, from $18 to $35 in a week, according to how hard I wanted to work; that is, in the city of Lynn. Today, on the same class of work, I would not be able, on any job in the city, to make over $15, and probably my wage would run nearer $12. That is based upon the experience of others that I know in the same kind of work. And another thing; where a man at that time would likely get eight or nine months' good work in a year, at the present time the season is shorter. Machinery is more largely used and of a more improved type. The manufacturers equip themselves to turn out their product in a shorter time, and the seasons of employment are shorter and more uncertain . . . I would like to state one instance of the development of machinery. In respect to the operation of nailing the heel on to the boot or shoe, fastening the heel in with nails, about fifteen years ago I remember working at a factory where that operation was done by hand in the original way. A man stood up with a hammer and nailed those heels on, and 100 to 125 pairs of that grade of work was considered a good day's work. Five years later it is done by what they call the National nailing machine, where a man and a boy did five times as much. That man and the boy did the work that it would require five men to do. . . .

Q. Taking the material as it is prepared for the shoemaker, how many hands does a gentleman's finished shoe pass through in the process of manufacture?

A. To answer that question in another way, there are about one hundred subdivisions of labor in the manufacture of a shoe, varying more or less according to the factory and methods and the kind of shoe made. There are different combinations of these subdivisions.

Q. Now, let me ask, in connection with that, what effect has that specializing, if it might be so termed, upon the workman? Has it a beneficial effect or otherwise?

A. Oh, it has been detrimental to the workman.

Q. The workman only knows how to perform the labor of one department?

A. That is all, and he becomes a mere machine. You know we have the piece work system almost entirely, and if we work for a week price, there is a stint that comes with it that makes it virtually a piecework system, and it has come to be a race with a man. Now, take the proposition of a man operating a machine to nail on forty to sixty pairs cases of heels in a day. That is 2,400 pairs, 4,800 shoes, in a day. One not accustomed to it would wonder how a man could pick up and lay down 4,800 shoes in a day, to say nothing of putting them on a jack into a machine and having them nailed on. That is the driving method of the manufacture of shoes under these minute subdivisions.

Q. Under that system of special work, has the general worker of today the same opportunity to go out into the world and make a living as you think he had before this method was introduced?

A. No.

Q. Are there many workmen in the factory who can make a whole shoe?

A. No, the art of shoemaking, so far as the individual is concerned, has got to be a thing of the past. About all the actual shoemakers you can find today are located in small cobbling and custom shops—old-time workmen; and almost invariably you will find that they are old men.

Q. If the workman is thrown out of employment in the factory, he has to seek some other factory and do just the identical work that he did in that factory?

A. Precisely.

Q. You have been in a position to observe the effect of this change on the workman as compared with the older system I have referred to. What effect, if any, has it had on the social habits of the workman, or have you noticed any?

A. I think it has had quite an effect. In Lynn today—I speak of Lynn as illustrative of other shoe centers—the city government is trying to agree upon a site for one of the old-time shoe factories. They are going to preserve it as an heirloom; a little factory about ten by fourteen, a little shop. In these old shops, years ago, one man owned the shop; he took in work and three, four, five, or six others, neighbors, came in there and sat down and made shoes right in their laps, and there was no machinery. Everybody was at liberty to talk; they were all politicians. . . . Of course, under these conditions, there was absolute freedom and exchange of ideas, they naturally would become more intelligent than shoe workers can at the present time, when they are driving each man to see how many shoes he can handle, and where he is surrounded by noisy machinery. And another thing, this nervous strain on a man doing just one thing over and over and over again must necessarily have a wearing effect on him; and his ideals, I believe, must be lowered.

Q. What are the hours of labor?

A. Ten hours a day almost uniformly.

Q. Any overtime work?

A. Very rarely. It is a very rare thing when a shoe manufacturer gets business enough to run overtime.

Q. What is the effect, generally speaking, of the employment of boys and girls in the factory?

A. That is quite an evil. I have seen small children standing on boxes because they were not tall enough to stand up to a man's work and operate machines; of course, not those kinds of machines that required the most skilled attention, but the introduction of child labor is quite a factor, sometimes displacing the head of the family. There was an instance in Marlboro where a man was receiving $2 a day; the firm turned him off and put in his own son at $1, at the same job.

A Currier (1879) *

If men work hard ten hours a day, their labor is really twelve; time in preparing, going to and returning from work, being at least two hours. Most men, after working hard all day, confined in a shop, need relaxation of mind and body; and few can use the short time they have in study, many trades being of an exhaustive nature. Machinery in my trade does not benefit the worker. It lessens the hand labor by one-half; while the finished article will, in looks and feeling (to use a trade term), be equal to the hand work; but the use of machinery on leather working destroys twenty-five per cent of its usefulness, as any currier can easily prove. Machinery prepares work for labor, or finishes it after, so men can run over work quickly without giving it the benefit needed. The market is glutted, and we have seasons of dullness; advantage is taken of men's wants, and the pay is cut down; our tasks are increased, and, if we remonstrate, we are told our places can be filled. I work harder now than when my pay was twice as large. Less than five years ago wages were from $12 to $18 a week currency; now they are from $6 to $12, and work not as steady. To show you how men are brought down, I will give a case of a shop in which are employed 100 to 125 men. During working hours the men are not allowed to speak to each other, though working close together, on pain of instant discharge. Men are hired to watch and patrol the shop. The workers of Massachusetts have always been law and order men; and (my knowledge goes no farther) the State and country were safe when they stood between them and danger. We loved the country, and respected the laws. For the last five years the times have been growing worse every year, until we have

* Massachusetts, Bureau of Statistics of Labor, *Tenth Annual Report* (Boston, 1879), p. 133.

been brought down so far that we have not much farther to go. What do the mechanics of Massachusetts say to each other? I will tell you: "We must have a change. Any thing is better than this. We cannot be worse off, no matter what the change is."

A Printer (1899) *

. . . I think that the opportunity for rising from the ranks of labor to the ranks of the employers has largely gone by. I do not mean to say wiped out entirely, but I mean to say largely eliminated. The man who set up a small printing office with a little job press and a few cases of type, and would go out and solicit work and make a little money out of it—that class of men is being rapidly eliminated. I was independent to the extent that as long as I had my trade I could earn my living, but today that is not true; and that character of men is wiped out almost entirely. The large printing office with its improved machinery makes it impossible for me to compete with them.

Q. You referred to the times when we were doing things by a limited amount of capital or machinery. Do you think it is possible for the world to go back again to the little boot and shoe shop and the little engine and the little boiler?

A. No.

Q. Has not the age of concentration and great capital and of large machinery come to stay, and have we not to seek for a remedy in some other direction than to try to eliminate this great body of capital and great body of machinery?

A. Undoubtedly; the organization does not stand for reactionists. We do not want to go back to the time when we could do without the sewing machine, or the machinery for manufacturing purposes, or the large aggregations of capital; but we do want our capital controlled in such a way that it will not result in the displacement of three-fourths of the population for the increased wealth of one-fourth of the population.

* From the testimony of Jacob G. Schonfarber, member of the International Typographical Union and the Knights of Labor, December 5, 1899. U.S. Congress, House, *Report of the Industrial Commission on the Relations and Conditions of Capital and Labor Employed in Manufactures and General Business,* 56th Cong., 2d Sess., House Doc. 495 (Washington: U.S. Government Printing Office, 1901), VII, 442.

LOSS OF STATUS

A Machinist (1883) *

By Mr. GEORGE:

Q. State your age, residence, and occupation.

A. I am about twenty-three years old; I live in this city; I am a machinist, and have been in that business about nine years.

Q. Do you work in a shop?

A. Yes, sir; I work in different shops.

CHANGED CONDITIONS—SUBDIVISIONS
OF THE TRADE

Q. Is there any difference between the conditions under which machinery is made now and those which existed ten years ago?

A. A great deal of difference.

Q. State the differences as well as you can.

A. Well, the trade has been subdivided and those subdivisions have been again subdivided, so that a man never learns the machinist's trade now. Ten years ago he learned, not the whole of the trade, but a fair portion of it. Also, there is more machinery used in the business, which again makes machinery. In the case of making the sewing machine, for instance, you find that the trade is so subdivided that a man is not considered a machinist at all. Hence, it is merely laborers' work and it is laborers that work at that branch of our trade. The different branches of the trade are divided and subdivided so that one man may make just a particular part of a machine and may not know anything whatever about another part of the same machine. In that way machinery is produced a great deal cheaper than it used to be formerly, and in fact, through this system of work, 100 men are able to do now what it took 300 or 400 men to do fifteen years ago. By the use of machinery and the subdivision of the trade they so simplify the work that it is made a great deal easier and put together a great deal faster. There is no system of apprenticeship, I may say, in the business. You simply go in and learn whatever branch you are put at, and you stay at that unless you are changed to another.

* From the testimony of John Morrison, August 28, 1883. U.S. Congress, Senate, *Report of the Committee of the Senate upon the Relations between Labor and Capital* (Washington: U.S. Government Printing Office, 1885), I, 755-759.

Q. Does a man learn his branch very rapidly?

A. Yes, sir; he can learn his portion of the business very rapidly. Of course he becomes very expert at it, doing that all the time and nothing else, and therefore he is able to do a great deal more work in that particular branch than if he were a general hand and expected to do everything in the business as it came along. . . .

Q. Have you noticed the effect upon the intellect of this plan of keeping a man at one particular branch?

A. Yes. It has a very demoralizing effect upon the mind throughout. The man thinks of nothing else but that particular branch; he knows that he cannot leave that particular branch and go to any other; he has got no chance whatever to learn anything else because he is kept steadily and constantly at that particular thing, and of course his intellect must be narrowed by it.

Q. And does he not finally acquire so much skill in the manipulation of his particular part of the business that he does it without any mental effort?

A. Almost. In fact he becomes almost a part of the machinery.

By the CHAIRMAN:

Q. Then if he gets so skilled that he has not to think about his work, why cannot he compose poetry, or give range to his imagination, or occupy his mind in some other way while he is at work?

A. As a rule a man of that kind has more to think of about his family and his belly than he has about poetry.

The CHAIRMAN. That is right.

By Mr. GEORGE:

Q. Has there been in the last ten or fifteen years any great revolution in the making of machinery so far as regards the capital that is required to start the business?

A. Well, I understand that at this present day you could not start in the machinist's business to compete successfully with any of these large firms with a capital of less than $20,000 or $30,000. That is my own judgment. There have been cases known where men started ten or fifteen years ago on what they had earned themselves, and they have grown up gradually into a good business. One of these firms is Floyd & Sons, on Twentieth Street. That man started out of his own earnings; he saved enough to start a pretty fair-sized shop, and he is occupying it today; but since that time it appears the larger ones are squeezing out the smaller, and forcing more of them into the ranks of labor, thus causing more competition among the workers.

DIFFICULTY OF RISING OUT OF THE
WAGE-WORKING CLASS

Q. What is the prospect for a man now working in one of these machine shops, a man who is temperate and economical and thrifty to become a boss or a manufacturer of machinery himself from his own savings? Could a man do it without getting aid from some relative who might die and leave him a fortune, or without drawing a lottery prize, or something of that sort?

A. Well, speaking generally, there is no chance. They have lost all desire to become bosses now.

Q. Why have they lost that desire?

A. Why, because the trade has become demoralized. First they earn so small wages; and, next, it takes so much capital to become a boss now that they cannot think of it, because it takes all they can earn to live.

Q. Then it is the hopelessness of the effort that produces the loss of the desire on their part; is that it?

A. That is the idea. . . .

SOCIAL CONDITIONS OF MACHINISTS IN NEW YORK

Q. What is the social condition of the machinists in New York and the surrounding towns and cities?

A. It is rather low compared to what their social condition was ten or fifteen years ago.

Q. Do you remember when it was better?

A. When I first went to learn the trade a machinist considered himself more than the average workingman; in fact he did not like to be called a workingman. He liked to be called a mechanic. Today he recognizes the fact that he is simply a laborer the same as the others. Ten years ago even he considered himself a little above the average workingman; he thought himself a mechanic, and felt he belonged in the middle class; but today he recognizes the fact that he is simply the same as any other ordinary laborer, no more and no less.

Q. What sort of houses or lodgings do the machinists occupy as a general rule?

A As a general rule they live in tenement houses, often on the top floor.

Q. How is it as to the size of the apartments that they occupy, the conveniences and comforts they afford, their healthfulness, the character of the neighborhood and the general surroundings?

A. That depends a great deal upon the size of the families. In most cases they are compelled to send their families to work, and of course they have to have rooms in proportion to the size of their families, and of course it often robs them of their earnings to pay rent; but as a rule the machinists live in the lowest quarters of the city, between Eighth and Eleventh Avenues, on the west side, and on the east side between Third Avenue and the river. You will find the machinists stuck in those quarters on both sides of the city.

TOO MANY MACHINISTS IN NEW YORK

One great trouble with our trade is that there is such a surplus of machinists in the market now that every day sees seven or eight at the door of every shop looking for a job. In fact they are denied the right to labor, and that is what we kick about. About two months ago, I believe there was about one-fifth of our trade in this city entirely out of work.

Q. Do you know from reading the papers or from your general knowledge of the business whether there are places in other cities or other parts of the country that those men could have gone and got work?

A. I know from general reports of the condition of our trade that the same condition existed throughout the country generally.

Q. Then those men could not have bettered themselves by going to any other place, you think?

A. Not in a body.

MACHINISTS HAVE SUNK FROM THE MIDDLE
TO THE LOWER CLASS

Q. I am requested to ask you this question: Dividing the public, as is commonly done, into the upper, middle, and lower classes, to which class would you assign the average workingman of your trade at the time when you entered it, and to which class would you assign him now?

A. I now assign them to the lower class. At the time I entered the trade I should assign them as merely hanging on to the middle class, ready to drop out at any time.

Q. What is the character of the social intercourse of those workingmen? Answer first with reference to their intercourse with other people outside of their own trade—merchants, employers, and others.

A. Are you asking what sort of social intercourse exists between the machinists and the merchants? If you are, there is none whatever, or very little if any.

Q. What sort of social intercourse exists among the machinists themselves and their families, as to visiting, entertaining one another, and having little parties and other forms of sociability, those little things that go to make up the social pleasures of life?

A. In fact with the married folks that has died out—such things as birthday parties, picnics, and so on. The machinists today are on such small pay, and the cost of living is so high, that they have very little, if anything, to spend for recreation, and the machinist has to content himself with enjoying himself at home, either fighting with his wife or licking his children.

Q. I hope that is not a common amusement in the trade. Was it so ten years ago?

A. It was not; from the fact that they then sought enjoyment in other places, and had a little more money to spend. But since they have had no organization worth speaking of, of course their pay has gone down. At that time they had a form of organization in some way or other which seemed to keep up the wages, and there was more life left in the machinist then; he had more ambition, he felt more like seeking enjoyment outside, and in reading and such things, but now it is changed to the opposite; the machinist has no such desires.

Q. What is the social air about the ordinary machinist's house? Are there evidences of happiness, and joy, and hilarity, or is the general atmosphere solemn, and somber, and gloomy?

A. To explain that fully, I would state first of all, that machinists have got to work ten hours a day in New York, and that they are compelled to work very hard. In fact the machinists of America are compelled to do about one-third more work than the machinists do in England in a day. Therefore, when they come home they are naturally played out from shoving the file, or using the hammer or the chisel, or whatever it may be, such long hours. They are pretty well played out when they come home, and the first thing they think of is having something to eat and sitting down, and resting, and then of striking a bed. Of course when a man is dragged out in that way he is naturally cranky, and he makes all around him cranky; so, instead of a pleasant house it is every day expecting to lose his job by competition from his fellow workman, there being so many out of employment, and no places for them, and his wages being pulled down through their competition, looking at all times to be thrown out of work in that way, and staring starvation in the face makes him feel sad, and the head of the house being sad, of course the whole family are the same, so the house looks like a dull prison instead of a home.

Q. Do you mean to say that that is the general condition of the machinists in New York and in this vicinity?

A. That is their general condition, with, of course, a good many exceptions. That is the general condition to the best of my knowledge.

INTIMIDATION AND "BLACKLISTING"
BY EMPLOYERS

Q. Where do you work?

A. I would rather not have it in print. Perhaps I would have to go Monday morning if I did. We are so situated in the machinist's trade that we daren't let them know much about us. If they know that we open our mouths on the labor question, and try to form organizations, we are quietly told that "business is slack," and we have got to go.

Q. Do you know of anybody being discharged for making speeches on the labor question?

A. Yes; I do know of several. A little less than a year ago several members of the organization that I belong to were discharged because it was discovered that they were members of the organization.

Q. Do you say those men were members of the same organization that you belonged to?

A. Yes, sir; but not working in the same place where I work. And in fact many of my trade have been on the "black list" and have had to leave town to find work.

CONDITIONS OF LABOR

Robert D. Layton (1883) *

Many of our strikes and difficulties with employers have resulted from obnoxious rules and regulations established in their works, although the majority of them have arisen from differences as to the wages that should be paid for labor.

Q. Can you give us some instances of the obnoxious rules of which you speak?

A. Yes; one instance was on the part of a large firm of carriage manufacturers at Rochester, N. Y.—James Cunningham, Sons & Co. Just a year ago this month their men rebelled against certain rules that they

* From the testimony of Robert D. Layton, Pittsburgh, Pennsylvania, Grand Secretary of the Knights of Labor, February 6, 1883. U.S. Congress, Senate, *Report of the Committee of the Senate upon the Relations between Labor and Capital* (Washington: U.S. Government Printing Office, 1885), I, 8-10.

had established in their works—rules degrading to human nature. For instance, the faucets in the water sinks were locked up, and when an employee wanted a drink of water he had to go to the foreman of his department and ask for a drink; the foreman went and unlocked the faucet and gave him a cupful of water, and whether that was enough to satisfy his thirst or not, it was all he got. When the men entered in the morning they were numbered by checks. A man lost his identity as a man and took a number like a prisoner in a penitentiary. The checks ran up to five hundred and something. If a man worked in the third or fourth story of the building (it was a large, high building), and if he was an old man—for they had a good many old men doing light work—when the bell rang for dinner he was obliged to walk down several pairs of stairs, take off his check and then walk up stairs again to eat his dinner, and when he got done he had to walk down again and put on the check before the bell rang for afternoon work. In that way they knew just when a man came in or went out. . . . Another obnoxious rule was that if a man was half or even a quarter of a minute late he was shut out. They had a gate and it would be shut down upon a man even when he was going in, sometimes so quickly that he would hardly have time to draw his foot back to keep it from being crushed by the gate, and that man would be kept out until nine o'clock, so that he would make only three-quarters of a day's work. The rule was that the men had to be *in* the works before the whistle blew.

Q. What was the hour at which they were required to be there?

A. Seven o'clock in the morning. Ten hours, I understand, was the length of a day's work there. These rules were exceedingly obnoxious to the men. . . . Our miners almost universally complain of being cheated in the amount of coal that they take out. That is another cause of great aggravation and disturbance. In some mines, they dig and get pay for the "run of the bank"—that is, slack and lump and nut coal all go in together at so much a ton. In other mines the miners are paid for simply the lump coal; and all the rest is deducted. The men have to dig the other kinds for nothing, getting so much a bushel for the lump coal only—coal that is . . . [too] . . . large to go through the screen. The size of the screen is regulated by law in Pennsylvania, but as you proceed in this investigation we will produce witnesses who will prove that the screens are often half an inch larger than the size the law prescribes. The screen is made of long bars of iron, and the coal runs down, over, and between them.

Q. And is the miner allowed only for that coal which is too large to pass through?

A. Yes, sir, the miner is allowed for that; the rest he loses; and in many instances the screens, as I have said, do not conform to the law, but are larger than the prescribed size. In such cases they let coal through that does not go into the weight below, and the miner loses that. It goes by default utterly, and there is a great deal of slack waste.

Q. I take it from what you say, then, that the miners are paid for the amount of coal which they dig?

A. Yes.

THE COMPANY STORE

A Massachusetts Quarryman (1879) *

There are eight companies in the stone business here, only four of which are running at present; and, running or loafing, they have a store apiece. All their employees must trade in their stores; if not, "get work where you trade. We keep as good articles here as you can get elsewhere, and sell as cheap too." And that is all the satisfaction you will get for your complaint. I have had to pay $1.35 for a pair of children's shoes that I could buy outside for 50 cents, and so on with everything else, to $2 on a barrel of flour; and everybody else must do likewise, i.e., those who work on stone. And that is not all either: some of them have tenement houses, and they must be kept full; and those who live in them are in a complete stage of vassalage. And that is not all: no matter how frugally you live, you never get anything ahead; and those having helpless families scarcely ever receive a dollar. They are closely watched on the books, lest they might overrun their wages; and consequently they will get nothing, only as they earn it. Such is the atrocious system here; and this is a part of free, enlightened Massachusetts! I suppose, if the workingman protested against this state of affairs, they'd be dubbed "communists," but no: their manhood is completely gone. They dare not murmur at it even, and is it any wonder? They have no means to better their condition; and it is, to say the least, deplorable.

* From the reply of a Massachusetts quarryman to a questionnaire of the Massachusetts Bureau of Statistics of Labor. Massachusetts, Bureau of Statistics of Labor, *Tenth Annual Report* (Boston, 1879), p. 124.

Samuel Gompers (1899) *

. . . There is not a case that I know of, or which has come under my observation in many years, where the people could not buy the things they needed from ten to twenty, and in some cases fifty per cent less in other stores than they were required to pay in the company's stores. The store-order system is in a measure a system of peonage, where a workman does not receive wages for his labor, but something in kind. A workman has a right to be paid his wages in the lawful money of the country, of which he can dispose to the best advantage, as he pleases. Under the store-order system the employers deduct from the wages the amount that the workers may be indebted to the store. This has led, first, to overcharging; secondly, to compulsion of purchase at the place, whether they desire it or not, and has encouraged the custom of over-charging, not only in the price of the article but frequently items are added which the workmen or their families have never had. I had oc-casion to go to Norwich, Connecticut, within the past few days, and there, in Taftville, Connecticut, a village four miles from the city limits, they have the store-order system, too, and the company houses, and weeks and weeks and months and a year has passed where the workmen have not received a dollar in wages. They are practically bound there; practically bound to the soil. They can not move; can not quit. Under the system they can not move; they are deprived of the right of American citizens, to move where they please. The strike there now is as much due to that as it is to an increase of wages—the strike of the textile workers there.

THE COMPANY TOWN

Pullman Strikers (1894) †

Mr. President and Brothers of the American Railway Union: We struck at Pullman because we were without hope. We joined the American

* From the testimony of Samuel Gompers, President of the American Fed-eration of Labor, April 18, 1899. U.S. Congress, House, *Report of the In-dustrial Commission on the Relations and Conditions of Capital and Labor Employed in Manufactures and General Business,* 56th Cong., 2d Sess., House Doc. 495 (Washington: U.S. Government Printing Office, 1901), VII, 614-615.

† From the Pullman Strikers' Statement at the Convention of the American Railway Union held in Uhlich Hall, Chicago, June 15, 1894. U.S. Congress, House, United States Strike Commission, *Report on the Chicago Strike of June-July, 1894* (Washington: U.S. Government Printing Office, 1895), pp. 87-88.

Railway Union because it gave us a glimmer of hope. Twenty thousand souls, men, women, and little ones, have their eyes turned toward this convention today, straining eagerly through dark despondency for a glimmer of the heaven-sent message you alone can give us on this earth.

In stating to this body our grievances it is hard to tell where to begin. You all must know that the proximate cause of our strike was the discharge of two members of our grievance committee the day after George M. Pullman, himself, and Thomas H. Wickes, his second vice-president, had guaranteed them absolute immunity. The more remote causes are still imminent. Five reductions in wages, in work, and in conditions of employment swept through the shops at Pullman between May and December, 1893. The last was the most severe, amounting to nearly thirty per cent, and our rents had not fallen. We owed Pullman $70,000 when we struck May 11. We owe him twice as much today. He does not evict us for two reasons: One, the force of popular sentiment and public opinion; the other because he hopes to starve us out, to break through in the back of the American Railway Union, and to deduct from our miserable wages when we are forced to return to him the last dollar we owe him for the occupancy of his houses.

Rents all over the city in every quarter of its vast extent have fallen, in some cases to one-half. Residences, compared with which ours are hovels, can be had a few miles away at the price we have been contributing to make a millionaire a billionaire. What we pay $15 for in Pullman is leased for $8 in Roseland; and remember that just as no man or woman of our 4,000 toilers has ever felt the friendly pressure of George M. Pullman's hand, so no man or woman of us all has ever owned or can ever hope to own one inch of George M. Pullman's land. Why, even the very streets are his. His ground has never been platted of record, and today he may debar any man who has acquiring rights as his tenant from walking in his highways. And those streets; do you know what he has named them? He says after the four great inventors in methods of transportation. And do you know what their names are? Why, Fulton, Stephenson, Watt, and Pullman.

Water which Pullman buys from the city at 8 cents a thousand gallons he retails to us at 500 per cent advance and claims he is losing $400 a month on it. Gas which sells at 75 cents per thousand feet in Hyde Park, just north of us, he sells for $2.25. When we went to tell him our grievances he said we were all his "children."

Pullman, both the man and the town, is an ulcer on the body politic. He owns the houses, the schoolhouses, and churches of God in the town he gave his once humble name. The revenue he derives from these, the wages he pays out with one hand—the Pullman Palace Car Company, he takes back with the other—the Pullman Land Association. He is able by this to bid under any contract car shop in this country. His competitors in business, to meet this, must reduce the wages of their men. This gives him the excuse to reduce ours to conform to the market. His business rivals must in turn scale down; so must he. And thus the merry war—the dance of skeletons bathed in human tears—goes on, and it will go on, brothers, forever, unless you, the American Railway Union, stop it; end it; crush it out.

U.S. Strike Commission on Pullman Rents (1895) *

If we exclude the aesthetic and sanitary features at Pullman, the rents there are from twenty to twenty-five per cent higher than rents in Chicago or surrounding towns for similar accommodations. The aesthetic features are admired by visitors, but have little money value to employees, especially when they lack bread. The company aims to secure six per cent upon the cost of its tenements, which cost includes a proportionate share for paving, sewerage, water, parks, etc. It claims now to receive less than four per cent. . . . The company makes all repairs, and heretofore has not compelled tenants to pay for them. Under the printed leases, however, which tenants must sign, they agree to pay for *all repairs* which are either necessary (ordinary wear and damages by the elements *not* excepted) or which the company *chooses* to make.

The company's claim that the workmen need not hire its tenements and can live elsewhere if they choose is not entirely tenable. The fear of losing work keeps them in Pullman as long as there are tenements unoccupied, because the company is supposed, as a matter of business, to give a preference to its tenants when work is slack. The employees, believing that a tenant at Pullman has this advantage, naturally feel some compulsion to rent at Pullman, and thus to stand well with management. Exceptional and necessary expert workmen do not share this feeling to the same extent and are more free to hire or own homes elsewhere. While reducing wages the company made no reduction in rents. Its position is that the two matters are distinct, and that none of the reasons urged as justifying wage reduction by it as an employer can be considered by the company as a landlord.

The company claims that it is simply legitimate business to use its position and resources to hire in the labor market as cheaply as possible and at the same time to keep rents up regardless of what wages are paid

* U.S. Strike Commission, *Report on the Chicago Strike of June-July, 1894* (Washington: U.S. Government Printing Office, 1895), pp. xxxv-xxxvi.

to its tenants or what similar tenements rent for elsewhere; to avail itself to the full extent of business depression and competition in reducing wages, and to disregard these same conditions as to rents. No valid reason is assigned for this position except simply that the company has the power and the legal right to do it.

ABSENTEE OWNERSHIP

On September 23, 1913, some 9,000 miners, along with their families and possessions, made their way from the camps of the Colorado Fuel and Iron Co. to tent colonies established by the United Mine Workers on leased land. Thus began a fifteen-month strike against the mine operators. Protesting the allegedly feudalistic conditions under which they lived and worked, the miners demanded union recognition, an eight-hour day, abolition of the company store system, and enforcement of state mining laws. Three previous strikes—in 1883, 1893, and 1903—had failed; ironically, the imported strikebreakers of 1903 had become the strikers of 1913.

The strike dramatically illustrated one of the concomitants of industrial change: absentee ownership. John D. Rockefeller, Jr., counted the Colorado Fuel and Iron Co. among his extensive holdings, although for ten years he had neither visited the property nor attended a directors' meeting. Selected managers exercised virtually absolute control, and they proceeded to prepare for war by turning the mine fields into an armed camp, ostensibly to protect mining property and "loyal" workers. On April 20, 1914—a day of infamy in labor annals—an armed battle broke out at Ludlow, the largest of the tent colonies, after militiamen had mounted a machine gun on a hill overlooking the town. Responsibility for firing the first shot was a matter of dispute. In any case, the militiamen made thorough work of Ludlow, set the tents afire, and captured and subsequently shot three of the strikers. Eleven children and two women who had sought refuge in a pit underneath the tents were found suffocated or burned to death.

The arrival of federal cavalry, dispatched by President Woodrow Wilson, ended the open warfare that followed the Ludlow "massacre." Attempts at federal mediation, however, failed as the mine operators, apparently with the approval of Rockefeller, rejected the President's recommendations (which had been based on the report of a special commission) and moved to end the strike in their own way. The miners were decisively defeated.

Against this background, the U.S. Commisssion on Industrial Relations made a thorough investigation of the Colorado strike, calling in representatives of the mine operators, the union, and the state and local governments. What follows is the testimony of John R. Lawson, a strike leader and member of the Executive Board of the United Mine Workers of America, January 29, 1915.

John R. Lawson (1915) *

The Commission on Industrial Relations was created to inquire into the underlying causes of industrial unrest. Speaking for the many thousands of men, women, and children who suffered through the recent coal strike in Colorado, I say to your honorable body that you can well afford to let the testimony of John D. Rockefeller, Jr., bring your investigation to an end. Out of his mouth came a reason for every discontent that agitates the laboring class in the United States today, and if remedies are provided for the injustices that he disclosed a long step will be taken away from industrial disturbance.

For more than ten years he has been a director of the Colorado Fuel & Iron Co., vested with what is virtually the power of life and death over 12,000 men and their families, for the isolated nature of the coal mining industry lends itself to an absolutism unknown in other activities. This power, let it be pointed out, came to him by no healthful process of struggle and achievement, but entirely through the fact that he was the son of his father. His huge control of men and money was, in effect, a gift that marked the attainment of his maturity.

In those first days, when he might have been expected to possess a certain enthusiasm in his vast responsibilities, Colorado was shaken by the coal strike of 1903-4. It is a matter of undisputed record that a mercenary militia, paid openly by the mine operators, crushed this strike by the bold violation of every known constitutional right that the citizen was thought to possess. Men were herded in bull pens like cattle, homes were shattered, the writ of habeas corpus suspended, hundreds were loaded on cars and dumped into the desert without food or water, others were driven over the snow of the mountain ranges, a governor elected by 15,000 majority was unseated, a man never voted on for that office was made governor, and when there came a thing called peace, the blacklist gave 6,000 miners the choice between starvation or exile. The Colorado Fuel & Iron Co. organized and led that attack on the

* U.S. Congress, Senate, *Final Report and Testimony Submitted to Congress by the Commission on Industrial Relations,* 64th Cong., 1st Sess., Senate Doc. 415 (Washington: U.S. Government Printing Office, 1916), VIII, 8004-8006.

liberties of freemen, and yet you heard from Mr. Rockefeller's own lips that he never inquired into the causes of the strike, the conduct of his executives or the fate of those who lost. So little interest did he take in the affair, so faint was the impression it made upon him, that he could not even answer your questions as to its larger facts.

To take the place of the banished workers, thousands were imported, and the extent of the company's dragnet for new material may be judged from the fact that over thirty languages and dialects have been spoken in the mines since 1904.

Ten years pass, and in 1913 Colorado is once more pushed to the verge of bankruptcy by another strike. Many strikebreakers of 1903, reaching the limit of human endurance, followed the example of those whose places they had taken, choosing hunger and cold in tents on the mountain side and plains in preference to a continuance of unbearable conditions in the mines. By actual count, the union was supporting 21,508 men, women, and children in the various colonies in January, 1914.

What course did Mr. Rockefeller pursue in connection with this upheaval of employees? His duty was clear, for he is on record with this admission, "I think it is the duty of every director to ascertain the conditions as far as he can, and if there are abuses, to right them." Putting their justice to one side, the fact remains that we claimed many abuses and cited them specifically.

The statute law of Colorado ordered a semimonthly pay day, check-weightmen so that we might not be cheated, the right to form unions, the eight-hour day, and payment in cash—not scrip. We charged that the Colorado Fuel & Iron Co. had violated these and other laws, and in addition we told of evil housing conditions, high rents, company-store extortions, saloon environment, armed guards, and the denial of freedom in speech, education, religion, and politics. When 12,000 men back up such claims by taking their wives and children into wind-swept tents, surely they would seem to be deserving of consideration.

Yet upon the stand, throughout three whole days this week, John D. Rockefeller, Jr., insisted that he was absolutely ignorant of every detail of the strike. He stated that he had not received reports on labor conditions, he could not tell within several thousands how many men worked for him in Colorado, he did not know what wages they received or what rent they paid, he had never considered what the proper length of a working day should be, he did not know what constituted a living wage, and, most amazing of all, he had never even read the list of grievances that the strikers filed with the governor of Colorado and gave to the world through the press. He did not know whether or not fifty per cent of his

employees worked twelve hours a day, and when asked whether or not
he considered twelve hours a day in front of a blast furnace to be a
hardship he answered that he was not familiar enough with the work to
judge. He did not know how many of his employees worked seven days
a week the year around, but judged that it would be a hardship, yet when
asked what part of a year could be worked under such conditions without
hardship, he refused to approximate an opinion.

He knew that there was a system by which injured men or their
families were compensated, yet he did not know what the system was,
and when a list was read showing the beggarly amounts paid to crippled,
mangled miners, he would say nothing but that they were not matters
that a board of directors would pass on. He did not know that his
company's control of the courts had resulted in a condition where not
one damage suit has been filed against it in years, and he did not know
that men were treated like criminals for daring to mention unionism. He
could not even define collective bargaining, nor had he ever made the
slightest study of the great union or its principles against which the
Colorado Fuel & Iron Co. threw its power and its millions. He expressed
himself in favor of unions and then proceeded to negative this belief by
refusing to answer affirmatively a number of questions that bore upon
the manner in which unionization could be achieved. Asked whether he
would vote to discharge an executive officer if it should be proved that
he had spent money to corrupt the electorate, he answered, "I should
want to know the conditions." He did not know what the capitalization
was of the subcompany that operates the mine stores or what it paid on
the investment.

He did not know that the company built special buildings for saloons,
charging high rental, or that church meetings were compelled to be held
near saloons, and that in some cases saloons were in close contact with
the schools. He knew that the company had maintained a sociological
department, but he did not know what its activities were, nor was he
aware that his officials dictated the appointment of our preachers and
schoolteachers, and exercised the right of discharge if they offended by
criticism. As an excuse for this amazing lack of knowledge, he insisted
that the board of directors had placed control of such matters in the
hands of J. F. Welbourn and L. M. Bowers and held them responsible
for wise and just administration of labor affairs. He admitted that, aside
from these two, he had knowledge of no others who would be responsible
for labor conditions.

On the witness stand, L. M. Bowers, who gave his residence as
Binghamton, N.Y., stated that he was concerned only with the finances
of the Colorado Fuel & Iron Co., and knew nothing of labor conditions.

J. F. Welbourn admitted that until his election to the presidency he had been concerned with the sales department, always in Denver, and that it was not his habit to visit the mines. They pointed to E. H. Weitzel as the man in charge of labor conditions, and Weitzel stated that while he did not visit all the camps "frequently" he got to them as often as he could. . . .

These, Messrs. Commissioners—this record of indifference respecting human life and human happiness—are vital causes of industrial discontent. An employer who is never seen, and whose power over us is handed down from man to man until there is a chain that no individual can climb; our lives and our liberties passed over as a birthday gift or by will; our energies and futures capitalized by financiers in distant cities; our conditions of labor held of less account than dividends; our masters too often men who have never seen us, who care nothing for us, and will not, or can not, hear the cry of our despair.

There is another cause of industrial discontent, and this, too, flows from a Rockefeller source. This is the skillful attempt that is being made to substitute philanthropy for justice. There is not one of these foundations now spreading their millions over the world in showy generosity that does not draw those millions from some form of industrial injustice. It is not their money that these lords of commercialized virtue are spending, but the withheld wages of the American working class.

I sat in this room and heard Mr. Rockefeller read the list of activities that his foundation felt calculated "to promote the well-being of mankind"—an international health commission to extend to foreign countries and peoples the work of eradicating the hookworm, ten millions for the bureau of municipal research, a retreat for migratory birds in Louisiana, $100,000 for the American Academy in Rome, the promotion of medical education and health in China, thirty-four millions for the University of Chicago, one million for the Belgians, $20,000 a year for widows' pensions in New York, the investigation of vice conditions in Europe, and thirty-four millions for a general education board. A wave of horror swept over me during that reading, and I say to you that that same wave is now rushing over the entire working class in the United States. Health for China, a refuge for birds, food for the Belgians, pensions for New York widows, university training for the elect, and never a thought or a dollar for the many thousands of men, women, and children who starved in Colorado, for the widows robbed of husbands, children of their fathers, by law-violating conditions in the mines, or for the glaring illiteracy of the coal camps. There are thousands of Mr. Rockefeller's ex-employees in Colorado today who wish to God that they were in Belgium to be fed or birds to be cared for tenderly.

II. Organization

Against a background of industrial consolidation and growing labor discontent, the modern trade union movement took shape. Skilled workers, while they still possessed an advantageous bargaining position, were among the first to organize, several of their unions dating back to the 1850's. But the most important period of organization coincided with the full impact of industrialization and the steady deterioration of the worker's position in American society. Between 1866 and 1936, in addition to the appearance of scores of local, state, and national craft and industrial unions, five major labor federations made their appeal to the organized and the unorganized: the National Labor Union (1866), the Knights of Labor (1869), the American Federation of Labor (1886), the Industrial Workers of the World (1905), and the Congress of Industrial Organizations (1936). Of the five, only two—the A.F of L. and the C.I.O. —were able to maintain themselves through periods of economic crisis, internal dissension, and strong employer opposition, and only one—the I.W.W.—based its appeal on the overthrow of capitalism.

In view of the violence that punctuated capital-labor relations in industrial America, it is somewhat remarkable that trade unionism generally remained a conservative force, content with immediate material gains and dedicated largely to middle-class goals and values. The Knights of Labor, for example, professed "the complete emancipation of the wealth producers from the thralldom and loss of wage slavery" but at the same time claimed "no conflict with legitimate enterprise; no antagonism to necessary capital." Putting this into practice, it deprecated strikes and radical agitation and sought economic salvation in producers' cooperatives, whereby every worker could someday become a capitalist. The more practical-minded American Federation of Labor had fewer illusions; it recognized the permanence of the working class and the increasing difficulty of escape from that status, discarded cooperative utopias for "pure and simple" unionism—the immediate improvement of wages, hours, and working conditions—and willingly employed the strike weapon to enforce collective bargaining and advance the economic

26

position of its own exclusive membership, confined as it was largely to skilled workers organized along craft lines. The A.F of L. adroitly guided by Samuel Gompers, made a business of trade unionism—and a relatively successful one at that. "The trade unions," Gompers explained in 1906, "are the business organizations of the wage earners, to attend to the business of the wage earners." The prevailing philosophy of American trade unionism was never more succinctly put.

To one group of workers, a small but vocal minority, the narrow-sighted view of the conservative, craft-oriented A.F. of L. demanded a more vigorous and radical labor organization. Such sentiment gave birth to the illustrious Industrial Workers of the World. For an organization which probably never exceeded 120,000 members, it had a most dramatic history and made an impact on the American labor movement. Repudiating capitalism and the "American Separation of Labor," the I.W.W. made its principal appeal to western miners, construction gangs, migratory harvest laborers, lumberjacks, cannery workers, and textile workers. "We are going down in the gutter," I.W.W. leader William "Big Bill" Haywood announced, "to get at the mass of workers and bring them up to a decent plane of living." During its relatively short existence, the I.W.W. conducted numerous strikes, including a dramatic and successful textile strike at Lawrence, Massachusetts; it introduced new strike tactics, such as the sit-down and mass picketing; it momentarily congested some California jails by deliberately violating city ordinances aimed at I.W.W. street speakers (who had stood outside employment agencies to warn workers against paying for jobs that were often either nonexistent or suspiciously short-lived); and it continued to press for a fundamental transformation of the economic order.

Although torn by internal dissension, bitterly opposed by A.F. of L. leaders, and subjected to severe employer and government attacks, the I.W.W. nevertheless demonstrated the need to organize the unorganized, and especially that growing army of unskilled industrial workers ignored by the craft-conscious A.F. of L. It was left to the Congress of Industrial Organizations in the 1930's to take up that challenge and move into the mass production industries—into automobiles, steel, electricity, aluminum, rubber, and meatpacking. Efforts to organize these workers provoked a new wave of industrial strife, much of it as violent as that of the late nineteenth century. But the C.I.O., although more receptive than the A.F. of L. to radical ideas and political action, stopped short of any fundamental criticism of the prevailing economic system; instead, it endorsed the reformist New Deal, aligned itself with the liberal wing of the Democratic Party, and joined with the A.F. of L. to obtain for its members a greater share of the benefits of capitalism. The final amalgamation of the two labor organizations in 1955 confirmed this basic identity of interests.

If the history of labor be recorded in terms of its trade organizations, it must of necessity overlook a majority of the American working population. Only a small fraction of workers belonged to trade unions, probably not exceeding ten per cent by 1914 and hardly more than thirty per cent by 1960. The persistence of employer opposition in some areas only partially explains these statistics. In recent years, the unions themselves have made little headway in their periodic organizing drives, especially in the South. For thousands of Negro workers, racial discrimination in the trade unions has precluded membership. Perhaps more ominous, new arrivals on the labor market, while willingly accepting those standards which the unions secured over many years, have tended to shy away from labor organizations, if given an opportunity to do so, or have swelled the army of the apathetic within organized labor. The growth of the disinterested has in turn subjected some unions to oligarchical control and made corruption easier; moreover, it has reduced the overall effectiveness of the labor movement, particularly its attempts to extend organization to new areas. For millions of workers, however, especially those still able to recall the bitter experiences which followed the first demands for recognition, organized labor has proven its value in constantly improving wages and conditions.

WHY ORGANIZE?

Cigar Makers' International Union of America (1864) *

Labor has no protection—the weak are devoured by the strong. All wealth and power center in the hands of the few, and the many are their victims and bondsmen. In all countries and at all times capital has been used to monopolize particular branches of business, until the vast and various industrial pursuits of the world are rapidly coming under the immediate control of a comparatively small portion of mankind, tending, if not checked by the toiling millions, to enslave and impoverish them.

Labor is the creator of all wealth, and as such the laborer is at least entitled to a remuneration sufficient to enable himself and family to

* Preamble to the Constitution of the Cigar Makers' International Union of America (organized in 1864). Reprinted in New York, *Third Annual Report of the Bureau of Statistics of Labor of the State of New York, for the Year 1885* (Albany, 1886), pp. 544-545.

enjoy more of the leisure that rightfully belongs to him, more social advantages, more of the benefits, privileges and emoluments of the world; in a word, all those rights and privileges necessary to make him capable of enjoying, appreciating, defending and perpetuating the blessings of modern civilization. Past experience teaches us that labor has so far been unable to arrest the encroachments of capital, neither has it been able to obtain justice from lawmaking power. This is due to a lack of practical organization and unity of action. "In union there is strength." Organization and united action are the only means by which the laboring classes can gain any advantage for themselves. Good and strong labor organizations are enabled to defend and preserve the interests of the working people. By organization we are able to assist each other in cases of strikes and lock-outs, sickness and death. And through organization only the workers, as a class, are able to gain legislative advantages.

No one will dispute the beneficial results attendant upon harmonious and intelligent action, and it is imperatively the duty of man to do all in his power to secure thorough organization and unity of action. In the performance of that duty we have formed the Cigar Makers' International Union of America, with a view to securing the organization of every cigar maker, for the purpose of elevating the material, moral and intellectual welfare of the craft by the following means:

1. By gratuitously furnishing employment.

2. By mutual pecuniary aid in case of strikes and lock-outs, sickness and death.

3. By advancing money for traveling.

4. By defending members involved in legal difficulties consequent upon the discharge of their official duties to the union.

5. By the issuing of a trade journal defending the interests of the union of the trade.

6. By using all honorable means to effect a national federation of trade unions.

7. By prevailing upon the Legislature to secure, first the prohibition of child labor under fourteen years of age; the establishment of a normal day's labor to consist of not more than eight hours per day for all classes; the abolition of the truck system, tenement house cigar manufacture, and the system of letting out by contract the convict labor in prisons and reformatory institutions; the legalization of trade unions and the establishment of bureaus of labor statistics.

Samuel B. Donnelly (1899) *

Where trade unions are the strongest they are looked upon as reputable organizations, and their officers and people who are interested in their welfare as respectable and good citizens. The growth of the trade union is not entirely due to the efforts of the trade unionists themselves in the work of organization, or in proselyting or preaching the gospel of trade unionism, but it is from the fact that capital in almost every case is tyrannical and unrelenting. A proper illustration would be a comparison of the conditions of the mill workers of the State of Massachusetts with the mill workers of the State of Georgia. We have in the State of Massachusetts a system of labor laws, a system of inspection of factories, bureau of labor statistics, board of mediation and arbitration, and compulsory education, limiting the age of children that can be employed in the factory. The capitalist who owns the factory in Massachusetts has been transferring his industry nearer to the cotton fields; and we find that, in the State of Georgia, where industrial conditions are not as good as in the State of Massachusetts, the man who has been subject in the State of Massachusetts to all these laws, has been living under them, has been putting rails around his machinery, has been boxing in his belting, has been refusing to employ in his factory a child under the age of fourteen years, and has been putting on every floor of his factory separate closets [toilets] for male and female labor, has been giving Saturday half holidays for his employees, and abolishing the company store and complying with the law of the State of Massachusetts—when he goes to the State of Georgia and transfers his business there he does not put any railing around his machinery; he does not box in his belting; he employs children nine, ten, or twelve years of age at wages as low as 15 or 20 cents per day, and works them from the time the light shines in the morning until it is dark at night; and in his factory he has no closets, no sanitary conditions, such as are required in the State of Massachusetts; he simply does as he pleases and acts in a most tyrannical and unChristian-like manner. There is nothing in the world that will protect the workers in those respects except organization. Through organization in the States of Massachusetts and New York these laws were enacted. In the State of New York the factory inspector visits a shop, and if there is a child there of doubtful age, that child is

* From the testimony of Samuel B. Donnelly, President of the International Typographical Union, May 9, 1899. U.S. Congress, House, *Report of the Industrial Commission on the Relations and Conditions of Capital and Labor Employed in Manufactures and General Business,* 56th Cong., 2d Sess., House Doc. 495 (Washington: U.S. Government Printing Office, 1901), VII, 280.

sent instantly home, and the proprietor is warned that if it is repeated he will be prosecuted; and it is a fact that proprietors of all sorts of establishments have been fined in the courts from $1 to $1,000 for violation of the State laws for regulation of factories and conditions of employment. When a man who has obeyed these laws goes to the State of Georgia he is utterly disregardful—he appears to be a man without any human sentiment or sympathy whatever.

Q. Is that the rule with all those who go there?

A. I do not think that it is the rule; but I say there are enough cases of that kind to create a feeling among the working classes favorable to organization and to make the work of the trade unions in this organization easier, and they come to us with open arms and say: "We want you to help us."

John A. O'Connell (1914) *

Mr. O'CONNELL. I might say, Mr. Chairman and members of the commission, that the subject of collective bargaining is a matter that the workers—it is the goal that the worker has hoped to reach all these years. He has reached it by perfecting a system of organization. He had been slipping for years without one, waiting for the employer, generally, out of the goodness of his heart, to do something for him, insofar as his hours of labor and wage conditions were concerned. But, I dare say, that had he not woke up and perfected an organization where he was able through this organization to deal collectively with the employer, he would still be in the same rut he was all of the years before organization took place. I might recite a few things to the commission in relation to my own vocation, that of a teamster. Previous to 1900 it was nothing for the employer to work the employee from twelve to eighteen hours per day. The maximum rate of pay at that time was $16 per week, as a maximum. The minimum to the boy that we rated not as an apprentice, but as a beginner in the business—because it generally takes a strong back, and a man that is not imbued with the strength and the health to go through with the program as outlined by the employer in the teaming industry is very soon and quietly dropped from the pay roll—that minimum ran as low as $3.50 or $4 a week. . . .

The teamsters today, through a system of organization, have advanced

* From the testimony of John A. O'Connell, a teamster and Secretary of the San Francisco Labor Council, September 3, 1914. U.S. Congress, Senate, *Final Report and Testimony Submitted to Congress by the Commission on Industrial Relations,* 64th Cong., 1st Sess., Senate Doc. 415 (Washington: U.S. Government Printing Office, 1916), VI, 5278, 5280, 5281.

their wages from that minimum of $4 to $12, and their maximum from $16 to $24, and reduced the working conditions to a ten-hour day, and no work on Sunday. . . .

They [several previous employer witnesses] said to you that we were not responsible; that the business agent was practically our god, our boss; that we had no conception; that we did not care for the employer at all. Nothing could be more ridiculous. You men sitting here, especially that know something of labor, that have been affiliated with the American Federation of Labor, members of this commission, know that there is nothing more ridiculous. . . .

They say, get rid of our officials and get rid of the business agent. Why did we bring about that system of having business agents and having a president and having a business manager or a business representative? We follow the footsteps of the employer. Who is the most successful employer, the most successful association of business today? Only the fellow that has perfected his system in every department, and he has got a manager at the head of every one of those departments. We don't take any umbrage at him to organize his association and import his secretary in here; we don't take any umbrage at that, certainly. And we deal with him.

But he takes serious objection to the business representative of our organization coming into his office and having the audacity to talk for the poor fellow that he has got working for him. They ought to go out and get the fellow off the wagon and bring him in. And you men know and so does everybody in this room know that men that work for a living haven't had the proud privilege to be enrolled as university students. They haven't got a university education; and the first complaint, if we do permit or allow the man to come in and represent himself, he has such a way of presenting his case that he is immediately branded as a hoodlum or something else by the employer because he doesn't indulge in that sweet-scented language that we learn in our universities.

John Mitchell (1914) *

Mr. MITCHELL. . . . In my judgment there can be no permanent prosperity to the workingmen, there can be no permanent industrial peace, until the principle is firmly and fully established that in industrial

* From the testimony of John Mitchell, member of the State Working Men's Compensation Commission of New York, formerly Vice-President of the A.F. of L. and President of the United Mine Workers of America, April 6, 1914. U.S. Congress, Senate, *Final Report and Testimony Submitted to Congress by the Commission on Industrial Relations*, 64th Cong., 1st Sess., Senate Doc. 415 (Washington: U.S. Government Printing Office, 1916), I, 413-414, 415; IX, 8061.

life the settlements of wages, hours of labor, and all the important conditions of work, are made between the employers and the workingmen collectively and not between employers and working men individually. The individual workman theoretically bargains with his employer as to the wages to be paid by his employer; but practically there is no bargaining. The individual workman must accept the wages and conditions of employment that are offered to him by his employer. It is a matter of no concern at all to an employer if one workingman refuses employment. He thinks nothing about it, because there is another workingman ready to take the job.

As a consequence of this system of individual bargaining, which is really nonunionism, the conditions of the best men in the industry are brought down, practically, to a level with those of the weakest men in the industry. Collective bargaining, of course, means that there shall be a uniform and minimum standard of wages and that there shall be uniform hours of labor. . . .

I know that in the industry with which I am best acquainted, the coal industry, collective bargaining has not only increased tremendously the earnings of the mine workers, but what is perhaps of more importance it has given the whole mining population a different and a better view of life. That is, instead of being, as they once were, a hopeless, despondent people, whose labor brought them less than that upon which they could live decently, they have become a hopeful people; they have got a different outlook; they regard this as "our country," a country in which they feel an interest, a country that means something to them.

Now, it has given them that feeling of justifiable independence; it has made them better men, better citizens, better fathers, given them better homes; it has meant education for their children, and it has meant, in most cases, a provision for their old age. . . .

Mr. THOMPSON. Do the conditions which exist in the contract field exist also in the fields where the union does not exist, and where there are no contracts; or what, in general, is the difference between the two fields, if you know?

Mr. MITCHELL. No; the conditions are not at all similar in the districts and States where the union is not established, and of course there is no contractual relation; I mean there is no collective bargaining in the nonunion fields. For instance, in nearly all the state of West Virginia, which is now the second coal-producing state in the United States, the men work under terms that are fixed by the mine owners absolutely, and that is true of a great many of the Southern states—of Alabama, parts of Tennessee, and parts of Kentucky—the mine owners fix the terms of employment as they do in most parts of Colorado and Utah and New

Mexico, and in parts of Pennsylvania there is what we call the West-moreland County, Pennsylvania, district, and in western Maryland the terms are entirely fixed by the mine owners. The wages in all of these districts that I speak of are much lower than they are in the fields where trade agreements are made, and the hours of labor are longer in the nonunion fields. . . .

It seems to me, gentlemen, I repeat, that there can be no permanent industrial peace until workingmen have the right and exercise the right to collectively bargain with their employers for the sale of their labor. It does not matter that the head of some great corporation may be generous, that he may desire to improve the conditions of the working people. The working people are not satisfied with those gifts and benefactions which are given to them by their employers. What they want is not gifts; they want independence; they want security in their jobs—that reasonable security that makes them feel that they may not be dismissed from their employment without good cause, and that they can not have in the absence of united action.

WHY STRIKE?

Samuel Gompers (1899) *

The working people find that improvements in the methods of production and distribution are constantly being made, and unless they occasionally strike, or have the power to enter upon a strike, the improvements will all go to the employer and all the injuries to the employees. A strike is an effort on the part of the workers to obtain some of the improvements that have occurred resultant from bygone and present genius of our intelligence, of our mental progress. We are producing wealth today at a greater ratio than ever in the history of mankind, and a strike on the part of workers is, first, against deterioration in their condition, and, second, to be participants in some of the improvements. Strikes are caused from various reasons. The employer desires to reduce wages and lengthen hours of labor, while the desire on the part of employees is to obtain shorter hours of labor and better wages, and better surroundings. Strikes establish or maintain the rights of unionism; that is,

* From the testimony of Samuel Gompers, President of the American Federation of Labor, November 20, 1899. U.S. Congress, House, *Report of the Industrial Commission on the Relations and Conditions of Capital and Labor Employed in Manufactures and General Business,* 56th Cong., 2d Sess., House Doc. 495 (Washington: U.S. Government Printing Office, 1901), VII, 605-606, 607-609.

to establish and maintain the organization by which the rights of the workers can be the better protected and advanced against the little forms of oppression, sometimes economical, sometimes political—the effort on the part of employers to influence and intimidate workmen's political preferences; strikes against victimization; activity in the cause of the workers against the blacklist. . . .

It required 40,000 people in the city of New York in my own trade in 1877 to demonstrate to the employers that we had a right to be heard in our own defense of our trade, and an opportunity to be heard in our own interests. It cost the miners of the country, in 1897, sixteen weeks of suffering to secure a national conference and a national agreement. It cost the railroad brotherhoods long months of suffering, many of them sacrificing their positions, in the railroad strike of 1877, and in the Chicago, Burlington, and Quincy strike, of the same year, to secure from the employers the right to be heard through committees, their representatives—that is, their committees of the organization to secure these rights. Workmen have had to stand the brunt of the suffering. The American Republic was not established without some suffering, without some sacrifice, and no tangible right has yet been achieved in the interest of the people unless it has been secured by sacrifices and persistency. After a while we become a little more tolerant to each other and recognize all have rights; get around the table and chaff each other; all recognize that they were not so reasonable in the beginning. Now we propose to meet and discuss our interests, and if we can not agree we propose in a more reasonable way to conduct our contests, each to decide how to hold out and bring the other one to terms. A strike, too, is to industry as the right that the British people contended for in placing in the House of Commons the power to close the purse strings to the Government. The rights of the British people were secured in two centuries— between 1500 and 1700—more than ever before, by the securing of that power to withhold the supplies; tied up the purse strings and compelled the Crown to yield. A strike on the part of workmen is to close production and compel better terms and more rights to be acceded to the producers. The economic results of strikes to workers have been advantageous. Without strikes their rights would not have been considered. It is not that workmen or organized labor desires the strike, but it will tenaciously hold to the right to strike. We recognize that peaceful industry is necessary to successful civilized life, but the right to strike and the preparation to strike is the greatest preventive to strikes. If the workmen were to make up their minds tomorrow that they would under no circumstances strike, the employers would do all the striking for them in the way of lesser wages and longer hours of labor.

Q. The whole philosophy is contest and conquest?

A. Except when there be like power on both sides; then it becomes reason, by the power on both sides; it then comes to reason rather than contest and conquest. . . .

Q. A distinguished witness who was before this commission several weeks ago said that no strike was ever lost; if the men didn't gain the point in the matter of wages, they gained more in bringing their grievances before the public. Is that the view you take of it?

A. I have tried to make the same point in another way; yes. The social results and the economic advantages are beyond measure; and yet, I say that it is the constant effort of our organization to prevent strikes. We want to secure the same beneficent results without cessation of industry or interruption of commerce, and that can only be done when the workers are organized and the employers are organized, and the effect of the possession of machinery, of labor machinery, on production and distribution is in itself power, is in itself organization. I do not pretend to say—nor do I wish any wrong inference to be drawn from any statement I might make—that, by the organization of labor, strikes will be entirely eliminated from our system of society, from industry and commerce. I do not believe that that is at all possible so long as men's interests are absolutely diverse.

THE AMERICAN FEDERATION OF LABOR:
"PURE AND SIMPLE" UNIONISM

Adolph Strasser (1883) *

Q. By Mr. Pugh: You are seeking to improve home matters first?

A. Yes, sir: I look first to the trade I represent; I look first to cigars, to the interests of men who employ me to represent their interests.

Q. I was only asking you in regard to your ultimate ends.

A. We have no ultimate ends. We are going on from day to day. We are fighting only for immediate objects—objects that can be realized in a few years.

Q. By Mr. Call: You want something better to eat and to wear, and better houses to live in?

* From the testimony of Adolph Strasser, President of the Cigar Makers' International Union of America and a founder of the American Federation of Labor, August 21, 1883. U.S. Congress, Senate, *Report of the Committee of the Senate upon the Relations between Labor and Capital* (Washington: U.S. Government Printing Office, 1885), I, 460.

A. Yes; we want to dress better and to live better, and become better off and better citizens generally.

Q. I see that you are a little sensitive lest it should be thought that you are a mere theorizer. I do not look upon you in that light at all.

A. Well, we say in our constitution that we are opposed to theorists, and I have to represent the organization here. We are all practical men.

G. W. Perkins (1899) *

Real trade-unionists are not pessimists; they are not theorists; they are opportunists. We ameliorate as we journey along to a better industrial system. Emancipation, I do not know what it is—that is, I will not attempt to say what the system will be, when it arrives. I am an evolutionary trade-unionist. I hold that the human family is growing better morally, physically, and mentally. While perhaps some may dispute that we are growing better morally and physically—although they can not successfully do so—none can dispute but that we are growing better mentally. That being true, I hold that it is my duty to do all that I possibly can for myself and my fellowman under present conditions; and if we are growing better mentally, that future generations will know better what they want and how to get it; and it is none of my business to say what that system shall be. I concern myself chiefly with the present, and in my view our duty is to do all that we possibly can for the hired man, for the workingman as we find him today and under conditions we find him. What emancipation means I will leave to future generations to decide.

The A.F. of L. and the Socialists: Samuel Gompers v. Morris Hillquit (1914) †

Mr. HILLQUIT. Now, . . . is it your conception, Mr. Gompers, or that of the Federation, that workers in the United States today receive the full product of their labor?

* From the testimony of G. W. Perkins, President of the Cigar Makers' International Union of America—A.F. of L., May 5, 1899. U.S. Congress, House, *Report of the Industrial Commission on the Relations and Conditions of Capital and Labor Employed in Manufactures and General Business,* 56th Cong., 2d Sess., House Doc. 495 (Washington: U.S. Government Printing Office, 1901), VII, 176-177.

† From the testimony of Samuel Gompers, President of the American Federation of Labor, cross-examined by Morris Hillquit, Socialist Party leader, May 22, 1914. U.S. Congress, Senate, *Final Report and Testimony Submitted to Congress by the Commission on Industrial Relations,* 64th Cong., 1st Sess., Senate Doc. 415 (Washington: U.S. Government Printing Office, 1916), II, 1526-1529.

Mr. GOMPERS. I think, but I am not quite so sure, that I know what you have in mind.

Mr. HILLQUIT. Do you understand my question?

Mr. GOMPERS. I think I do, but in the generally accepted sense of that term, no.

Mr. HILLQUIT. In any particular sense, yes?

Mr. GOMPERS. No.

Mr. HILLQUIT. Then the workers of this country do not receive the whole product of their labor? Can you hazard a guess as to what proportion of the product they do receive in the shape of wages? . . .

Mr. GOMPERS. I will say that it is impossible for anyone to definitely say what proportion the workers receive as the result of their labor; but it is the fact that due to the organized-labor movement they have received and are receiving a larger share of the product of their labor than they ever did in the history of modern society.

Mr. HILLQUIT. Then one of the functions of organized labor is to increase the share of the workers in the product of their labor, is that correct?

Mr. GOMPERS. Yes, sir; organized labor makes constantly increasing demand upon society for reward for the services which the workers give to society, and without which the civilized life would be impossible.

Mr. HILLQUIT. And these demands for an increasing share of the reward of the product of labor continue by a gradual process all the time?

Mr. GOMPERS. I am not so sure as to gradual process. Sometimes it is not a gradual process, but it is all the time.

Mr. HILLQUIT. All the time?

Mr. GOMPERS. Yes, sir.

Mr. HILLQUIT. Then, Mr. Gompers, you assume that the organized labor movement has generally succeeded in forcing a certain increase of that portion of the workers in the share of the general product, do you?

Mr. GOMPERS. Yes, sir.

Mr. HILLQUIT. And it demands more now?

Mr. GOMPERS. Yes, sir.

Mr. HILLQUIT. And if it should get, say, 5 per cent more within the next year, will the organized labor movement rest contented with that and stop?

Mr. GOMPERS. Not if I know anything about human nature.

Mr. HILLQUIT. Will the organized labor movement, or the labor movement of the country generally, stop in its demands for an ever greater share in the product at any time before it has received or does receive the full product, and before in its eyes complete social justice shall have been done?

Mr. GOMPERS. That question again that you have bobbed up with quite serenely in regard to the share of the product of labor, say that the working people—and I prefer to say working people and speak of them as real human beings—the working people, as all other people, they are prompted by the same desires and hopes of a better life, and they are not willing to wait until after they have shuffled off this mortal coil for the better life, they want it here and now, and they want to make conditions better for their children so that they may meet the other, the newer problems in their time. The working people are pressing forward, pressing forward, making their claims and presenting those claims with whatever power they have, to exercise it in a normal, rational manner, to secure a larger, and constantly larger share of the products. They are working to the highest and best ideals of social justice.

Mr. HILLQUIT. Now, the highest and best ideals of social justice, as applied to the distribution of wealth, wouldn't that be a system under which the workers, manual, mental, directive, executive and all other lines together get the sum total of all the products we supply them?

Mr. GOMPERS. Really, a fish is caught by the tempting bait: a mouse or a rat is caught in a trap by the tempting bait; the intelligent, comprehensive, common-sense workmen prefer to deal with the problems of today, the problem which confronts them today, with which they are bound to contend if they want to advance, rather than to deal with a picture and a dream which has never had, and I am sure never will have, any reality in the affairs of humanity, and which threaten, if it could be introduced, the worst system of circumscriptional effort and activity that has ever been invented by the ken of the human kind.

Mr. HILLQUIT. That is what I want to get from you, Mr. Gompers, but I would like to get an answer. In your experience with the labor movement and in its ever forward march toward greater and greater improvement, and a greater and greater share of social justice, can you point out any line where the labor movement will stop and rest contented so long as it may receive short of the full product of its work?

Mr. GOMPERS. I say that the workers, as human beings, will never stop in any effort, nor stop at any point in the effort to secure greater improvements in their condition, a better life in all its phases. And wherever that may lead, whatever that may be, so far in my time and my age I decline to permit my mind or my activities to be labeled by any particular ism.

Mr. HILLQUIT. Do not try to attach any ism to me, please; but the question I ask is whether you maintain—whether the American Federation of Labor, and its authorized spokesmen have a general social philosophy, or work blindly from day to day?

Mr. GOMPERS. I think your question—

Mr. HILLQUIT. (interrupting). Inconvenient.

Mr. GOMPERS. No. I will tell you what it is, it is a question prompted to you, and is an insult.

Mr. HILLQUIT. It is not a question prompted to me.

Mr. GOMPERS. It is an insult.

Mr. HILLQUIT. Why? Why, Mr. Gompers?

Mr. GOMPERS. To insinuate that the men and women in the American Federation of Labor movement are acting blindly from day to day.

Mr. HILLQUIT. I have not insinuated—

Mr. GOMPERS. (interrupting). Your question implies it.

Mr. HILLQUIT. I am giving you an opportunity to deny.

Mr. GOMPERS. If a man should ask me whether I still beat my wife, any answer I could make would incriminate me if I answered yes or no. If I answered that I did not, the intimation would be that I had stopped. If I answered that I did, that I was continuing to beat her.

Mr. HILLQUIT. But Mr. Gompers, this question bears no analogy to that story—

Mr. GOMPERS (interrupting). Your question is an insult and a studied one.

Mr. HILLQUIT. Now, will you state whether you will or whether you will not answer my question?

Mr. GOMPERS. Will you repeat the question?

Mr. HILLQUIT. My question was whether the American Federation of Labor as represented by its spokesmen has a general social philosophy, or whether the organization is working blindly from day to day? Now, that is a plain question.

Mr. GOMPERS. Yes; it is a plain question; it is a plain insult.

Chairman WALSH. Do you refuse to answer it on the ground that it is insulting?

Mr. GOMPERS. Yes, sir.

Chairman WALSH. That is all, then.

Mr. HILLQUIT. Then, inform me upon this matter: In your political work of the labor movement is the American Federation of Labor guided by a general social philosophy, or is it not?

Mr. GOMPERS. It is guided by the history of the past, drawing its lessons from history, to know of the conditions by which the working people are surrounded and confronted; to work along the lines of least resistance; to accomplish the best results in improving the condition of the working people, men and women and children, today and tomorrow and tomorrow—and tomorrow's tomorrow; and each day making it a better day than the one that had gone before. That is the guiding principle and philosophy and aim of the labor movement—in order to secure a better life for all.

Mr. HILLQUIT. But in these efforts to improve conditions from day to day you must have an underlying standard of what is better, don't you?

Mr. GOMPERS. No. You start out with a given program, and everything must conform to it; and if the facts do not conform to your theories, why, your declarations, or, rather, your actions, betray the state of mind "so much the worse for the facts."

Mr. HILLQUIT. Mr. Gompers, what I ask you is this: You say you try to make the conditions of the workers better every day. In order to determine whether the conditions are better or worse you must have some standards by which you distinguish the bad from the good in the labor movement, do you not?

Mr. GOMPERS. Certainly. Well, is that—

Mr. HILLQUIT (interrupting). Now, just—

Mr. GOMPERS (interrupting). Well, one moment. Does it require much discernment to know that a wage of $3 a day and a workday of 8 hours a day in sanitary workshops are all better than $2.50 a day and 12 hours a day and under perilous conditions of labor? It does not require much conception of a social philosophy to understand that.

Mr. HILLQUIT. Then, Mr. Gompers, by the same parity of reasoning, $4 a day and seven hours a day of work and very attractive working conditions are still better?

Mr. GOMPERS. Unquestionably.

Mr. HILLQUIT. Therefore—

Mr. GOMPERS (interrupting). Just a moment. I have not stipulated $4 a day or $8 a day or any number of dollars a day or eight hours a day or seven hours a day or any number of hours a day, but the best possible conditions obtainable for the workers is the aim.

Mr. HILLQUIT. Yes; and when these conditions are obtained—

Mr. GOMPERS (interrupting). Why, then, we want better.

Mr. HILLQUIT (continuing). You will still strive for better?

Mr. GOMPERS. Yes.

Mr. HILLQUIT. Now, my question is, Will this effort on the part of organized labor ever stop until it has the full reward for its labor?

Mr. GOMPERS. It won't stop at all.

Mr. HILLQUIT. That is a question—

Mr. GOMPERS (interrupting). Not when any particular point is reached, whether it be that toward which you have just declared or anything else. The working people will never stop—

Mr. HILLQUIT. Exactly.

Mr. GOMPERS (continuing). In their effort to obtain a better life for themselves and for their wives and for their children and for humanity.

Mr. HILLQUIT. Then, the object of the labor union is to obtain complete social justice for themselves and for their wives and for their children?

Mr. GOMPERS. It is the effort to obtain a better life every day.

Mr. HILLQUIT. Every day and always—

Mr. GOMPERS. Every day. That does not limit it.

Mr. HILLQUIT. Until such time—

Mr. GOMPERS. Not until any time.

Mr. HILLQUIT. In other words—

Mr. GOMPERS (interrupting). In other words, we go further than you. (Laughter and applause in the audience.) You have an end; we have not.

THE INDUSTRIAL WORKERS OF THE WORLD: REVOLUTIONARY UNIONISM

Preamble of the I.W.W. (1908) *

The working class and the employing class have nothing in common. There can be no peace so long as hunger and want are found among millions of working people and the few, who make up the employing class, have all the good things of life.

Between these two classes a struggle must go on until the workers of the world organize as a class, take possession of the earth and the machinery of production, and abolish the wage system.

We find that the centering of the management of industries into fewer and fewer hands makes the trade unions unable to cope with the ever growing power of the employing class. The trade unions foster a state of affairs which allows one set of workers to be pitted against another set of workers in the same industry, thereby helping defeat one another in wage wars. Moreover, the trade unions aid the employing class to mislead the workers into the belief that the working class have interests in common with their employers.

These conditions can be changed and the interest of the working class upheld only by an organization formed in such a way that all its members in any one industry, or in all industries if necessary, cease work whenever a strike or lockout is on in any department thereof, thus making an injury to one an injury to all.

* As amended at the convention of 1908. Reprinted in I.W.W., *Songs of the Workers* (29th ed.: Chicago: Industrial Workers of the World, 1956.

Instead of the conservative motto, "A fair day's wage for a fair day's work," we must inscribe on our banner the revolutionary watchword, "Abolition of the wage system."

It is the historic mission of the working class to do away with capitalism. The army of production must be organized, not only for the everyday struggle with capitalists, but also to carry on production when capitalism shall have been overthrown. By organizing industrially we are forming the structure of the new society within the shell of the old.

William D. Haywood (1915) *

Mr. HAYWOOD. . . . . There are workers who have come to the conclusion that there is only one way to win this battle. We don't agree at all with the statement that you heard reiterated here day after day—that there is an identity of interests between capital and labor. We say to you frankly that there can be no identity of interests between labor, who produces all by their own labor power and their brains, and such men as John D. Rockefeller, Morgan, and their stockholders, who neither the industries that they own. We say that this struggle will go on in by brain or muscle or by any other effort contribute to the productivity of spite of anything that this commission can do or anything that you may recommend to Congress; that the struggle between the working class and the capitalistic class is an inevitable battle; that it is a fight for what the capitalistic class has control of—the means of life, the tools and machinery of production. These, we contend, should be in the hands of and controlled by the working class alone, independent of anything that capitalists and their shareholders and stockholders may say to the contrary.

Personally I don't think that this can be done by political action. . . .

Commissioner O'CONNELL. Have you in mind some other method by which it can?

Mr. HAYWOOD. Yes, sir; I think it can be done by direct action. I mean by organization of the forces of labor. Take, for instance, the organization that you know, the United Mine Workers of America. They have about one-half of the miners of this country organized. At least a sufficient number to control them all. I think the United Mine Workers can say to the mine owners, "You must put these mines in order, in proper shape, or we won't work in them." They can compel the intro-

---

* From the testimony of William D. Haywood, a founder and National Secretary-Treasurer of the I.W.W., May 12, 1915. U.S. Congress, Senate, *Final Report and Testimony Submitted to Congress by the Commission on Industrial Relations*, 64th Cong., 1st Sess., Senate Doc. 415 (Washington: U.S. Government Printing Office, 1916), XI, 10574-10575, 10582-10583.

duction of safety appliances, of ventilation systems, and save in that way thousands of lives every year. I don't think anybody will deny that they have that power to bring about that improvement. If they have the power to do that by direct action, they have the power to reduce their hours; they have the power to increase or at least to better the laboring conditions around the mines and have better houses. It seems to me there is no reason in the world why the miner should not enjoy, even in a mining camp, some of the advantages that the worker has in the city. And I think that free organization of miners, organized in one big union, having no contract with the boss, have no right to enter into a contract with the employer or any other combination of labor, to my mind. There can be each division of industry, each subdivision, be brought into a whole, and that will bring about the condition that I have described to you.

Commissioner O'CONNELL. You mean by that, by these economic organizations they would create, or control questions of hours and things of that kind you spoke of, but as to the ownership, the right of ownership, what is the method that you have in mind of your organization in connection with the method of taking over?

Mr. HAYWOOD. Taking over through the organization. If you are strong enough to compel the things I say, you are strong enough to say, "Here, Mr. Stockholder, we won't work for you any longer. You have drawn dividends out of our hides long enough; we propose that you shall go to work now, and under the same opportunities that we have had."

Commissioner O'CONNELL. Well, you propose by your strength and numbers to declare ownership?

Mr. HAYWOOD. Yes, exactly; through the efforts of the working class. . . .

Commissioner WEINSTOCK. Now, will you tell this commission, Mr. Haywood, as an authority on the subject, wherein, assuming that you and the Socialists and the American Federationists have the same objective in mind; that is, the betterment of the worker—will you point out to this commission as clearly and concisely as you can wherein your methods differ and are better than the method of the Socialists, and of the American Federationists? . . .

Mr. HAYWOOD. Without saying—without criticizing trade-unions, which I regard as having accomplished great good in their time, there are many things in the workings of trade-unions where they recognize the right of the bosses. The Industrial Workers of the World do not recognize that the bosses have any rights at all. We have founded the organization on the basis of the class struggle, and on that basis it must work out its ultimate.

The trade-union says, "Well, the boss has some right here, and we are going to enter into a contract with him." How long is it going to take to solve this problem if you have continuity of contracts? That is the thing we say.

The trade-union is organized on the basis of the tools they work with. Now, the tools are changing, and it is driving trade-unions out of business. For instance, the glass blowers—glass was made by workmen who blew through a tube. A glass maker, a glass blower himself contrived a machine whereby this blowing is done automatically, and the glass blower, he is wheeling sand to that machine now.

We believe that everybody that works around that machine ought to be organized just as before; we believe that everybody that works around the glass factory ought to be organized, organized with regard to the welfare of each other. . . .

Commissioner WEINSTOCK . . . I gather, then, from your statement that the two fundamental points in which I.W.W.'s differ from American Federationists is you are opposed to contracts with employers on the one hand, and you believe in one great union instead of craft unions. . . .

Mr. HAYWOOD. Can you conceive of anything that labor can not do if they were organized in one big union? If labor was organized and self-disciplined it could stop every wheel in the United States tonight—every one—and sweep off your capitalists and State legislatures and politicians into the sea. Labor is what runs this country, and if they were organized, scientifically organized—if they were class-conscious, if they recognized that the worker's interest was every worker's interest, there is nothing but what they can do.

Commissioner WEINSTOCK. Granting an organization so colossal in its character would have great power for good, would it not have great power for ill?

Mr. HAYWOOD. Yes, it would have great power for ill—that is, it would be ill for the capitalists. Every one of them would have to go to work.

Commissioner WEINSTOCK. Would it not also have great power in doing this—in establishing a new slavery? If the wage earner claims that under [the] present system of things he is in slavery, would not the colossal power of your plan simply be slavery with new masters?

Mr. HAYWOOD. Such a labor organization would be a fine sort of slavery. I would like to work for my union in a shop that I owned best.

Commissioner WEINSTOCK. If you were the "big Injun" chief?

Mr. HAYWOOD. No; to go right back in the mine that I came from. That is the place that I would like to go, right tomorrow, and receive for my labor, without any stockholder, without any Rockefeller taking off any part of it, the social value of what my labor contributed to society.

Commissioner WEINSTOCK. To that degree, then, I take it, the I.W.W.'s are Socialistic?

Mr. HAYWOOD. All right.

Commissioner WEINSTOCK. Let me see if I understand the distinction correctly between socialism and I.W.W.'ism.

As I understand it, I.W.W.'ism is socialism with this difference—

Mr. HAYWOOD (interrupting). With its working clothes on.

Joe Hill: I.W.W. Songwriter (1882-1915)

The I.W.W. sang its way to glory—and to eventual oblivion. But the demise of the organization, after the 1918 trial of 101 Wobbly leaders for subversive activities, did not diminish the popularity of several of the songs it inspired; and its most illustrious and prolific song writer was unquestionably the Swedish immigrant, Joel Emmanuel Hagglund— known as Joe Hill. Arrested in Salt Lake City in January 1914 on a murder charge, he was executed nearly two years later by a Utah firing squad. His guilt or innocence has long been disputed, even in labor circles, as have his dying words—"Don't waste time mourning. Organize." Nevertheless, he died an I.W.W. hero. Befitting the cause to which he was attached, Hill's funeral procession in Chicago attracted 30,000 sympathizers, and, as he requested, his body was cremated, the ashes placed into thirty envelopes and sent to all parts of the world—to all, that is, but the State of Utah because Joe Hill "did not want to be found dead there."

There Is Power in a Union*

by Joe Hill

(Tune: "There Is Power in the Blood")

Would you have freedom from wage slavery,
    Then join in the grand Industrial band;

* "There Is Power in a Union" by Joe Hill. From I.W.W., *Songs of the Workers* (29th ed.; Chicago: Industrial Workers of the World, 1956), p. 8. Reprinted by permission.

Would you from mis'ry and hunger be free,
Then come! Do your share, like a man.

CHORUS

There is pow'r, there is pow'r
In a band of workingmen,
When they stand hand in hand,
That's a pow'r, that's a pow'r
That must rule in every land—
One Industrial Union Grand.

Would you have mansions of gold in the sky,
And live in a shack, way in the back?
Would you have wings up in heaven to fly,
And starve here with rags on your back?

If you've had "nuff" of "the blood of the lamb"
Then join in the grand Industrial band;
If, for a change, you would have eggs and ham,
Then come, do your share, like a man.

If you like sluggers to beat off your head,
Then don't organize, all unions despise,
If you want nothing before you are dead,
Shake hands with your boss and look wise.

Come, all ye workers, from every land,
Come, join in the grand Industrial band,
Then we our share of this earth shall demand.
Come on! Do your share, like a man.

Casey Jones—the Union Scab*

(Tune: "Casey Jones")

The Workers on the S.P. line to strike sent out a call;
But Casey Jones, the engineer, he wouldn't strike at all;

* "Casey Jones—the Union Scab" by Joe Hill. From I.W.W., *Songs of the Workers* (29th ed., Chicago: Industrial Workers of the World, 1956), pp 46-47. Reprinted by permission.

His boiler it was leaking, and its drivers on the bum,
And his engine and its bearings, they were all out of plumb.

CHORUS

Casey Jones kept his junk pile running;
Casey Jones was working double time;
Casey Jones got a wooden medal,
For being good and faithful on the S.P. line.

The workers said to Casey: "Won't you help us win this strike?"
But Casey said: "Let me alone, you'd better take a hike."
Then Casey's wheezy engine ran right off the worn-out track,
And Casey hit the river with an awful crack.

Casey Jones hit the river bottom;
Casey Jones broke his blooming spine,
Casey Jones was an Angeleno,
He took a trip to heaven on the S.P. line.

When Casey Jones got up to heaven to the Pearly Gate,
He said: "I'm Casey Jones, the guy that pulled the S.P. freight."
"You're just the man," said Peter, "our musicians went on strike;
You can get a job a-scabbing any time you like."

Casey Jones got a job in heaven;
Casey Jones was doing mighty fine;
Casey Jones went scabbing on the angels,
Just like he did to workers on the S.P. line.

The angels got together, and they said it wasn't fair,
For Casey Jones to go around a-scabbing everywhere,
The Angel Union No. 23, they sure were there,
And they promptly fired Casey down the Golden Stair.

Casey Jones went to Hell a-flying.
"Casey Jones," the Devil said, "Oh fine;
Casey Jones, get busy shoveling sulphur—
That's what you get for scabbing on the S.P. line."

THE CONGRESS OF INDUSTRIAL
ORGANIZATIONS: INDUSTRIAL UNIONISM

Although the A.F. of L. managed to survive the Open Shop and Corporate Paternalism drives of the 1920's, its narrow definition of trade unionism precluded the organization of a rapidly growing army of workers in the mass production industries. In the early 1930's, however, a group of A.F. of L. leaders, including United Mine Workers' chief John L. Lewis, moved to alter this traditional craft-oriented policy in order to organize the new mass industries along industrial lines. Workers in many of the modern factories, they pointed out, performed in a single day tasks which might well bring them within the jurisdiction of several craft unions.

But the Gompers tradition proved difficult to change. Fearing serious inroads into their dues-paying membership and a curtailment of their jurisdiction, most of the major craft unions opposed industrial organization and, in the showdown fight at the 1935 national convention, defeated a minority report which would have permitted it within the A.F. of L. Before the convention ended, in a heated and perhaps symbolic exchange, Lewis caught the bulky carpenters' boss William L. Hutchison with a right fist and sent him crashing against a table. The next day plans were underway to form a Committee for Industrial Organization, which proved to be the nucleus of the Congress of Industrial Organizations.

Minority Report of Resolutions Committee on
Organization Policies: A.F. of L.
Convention (1935) *

During the fifty-five years the American Federation of Labor has existed its declared purpose has been to organize the unorganized industrial workers of the nation. The contributions from its numerous affiliates have been made in the belief that organization would be advanced for the purpose of adding economic strength to the various units and that the organization policies would at all times be molded to accomplish the main purpose of organizing the unorganized workers in the industrial field.

* American Federation of Labor, Resolutions Committee on Organization Policies, *Report of Proceedings of the Fifty-fifth Annual Convention of the American Federation of Labor Held at Atlantic City, New Jersey, October 7 to 19, Inclusive 1935* (Washington, 1935), pp. 523-524.

During the existence of the American Federation of Labor and since the date many of the charters were granted to National and International Unions upon craft lines, the changes in industrial methods have been such that the duties of millions of industrial workers are of a nature that did not exist at the time many National and International charters were issued. This makes it apparent that jurisdiction over these new classes of work could not have been anticipated and included in the jurisdictional outlines of charters issued to National and International Unions at a time when the work that is now performed by these millions of industrial workers did not exist.

We refuse to accept existing conditions as evidence that the organization policies of the American Federation of Labor have been successful. The fact that after fifty-five years of activity and effort we have enrolled under the banner of the American Federation of Labor approximately three and one-half millions of members of the thirty-nine millions of organizable workers is a condition that speaks for itself.

We declare the time has arrived when common sense demands the organization policies of the American Federation of Labor must be molded to meet present day needs. In the great mass production industries and those in which the workers are composite mechanics, specialized and engaged upon classes of work which do not fully qualify them for craft union membership, industrial organization is the only solution. Continuous employment, economic security and the ability to protect the individual workers depends upon organization upon industrial lines.

In those industries where the work performed by a majority of the workers is of such nature that it might fall within the jurisdictional claim of more than one craft union, or no established craft union, it is declared that industrial organization is the only form that will be acceptable to the workers or adequately meet their needs. Jurisdictional claims over small groups of workers in these industries prevent organization by breeding a fear that when once organized the workers in these plants will be separated, unity of action and their economic power destroyed by requiring various groups to transfer to National and International Unions organized upon craft lines.

To successfully organize the workers in industrial establishments where conditions outlined herein obtain there must be a clear declaration by the American Federation of Labor. It must recognize the right of these workers to organize into industrial unions and be granted unrestricted charters which guarantee the right to accept into membership all workers employed in the industry or establishment without fear of being compelled to destroy unity of action through recognition of jurisdictional claims made by National or International Unions.

It is not the intention of this declaration of policy to permit the taking away from National or International craft unions any part of their present membership, or potential membership in establishments where the dominant factor is skilled craftsmen coming under a proper definition of the jurisdiction of such National or International Unions. However, it is the declared purpose to provide for the organization of workers in mass production and other industries upon industrial and plant lines, regardless of claims based upon the question of jurisdiction.

The Executive Council of the American Federation of Labor is expressly directed and instructed to issue unrestricted charters to organizations formed in accordance with the policy herein enunciated. The Executive Council is also instructed to enter upon an aggressive organization campaign in those industries in which the great mass of the workers are not now organized, issue unrestricted charters to workers organized into independent unions, company-dominated unions, and those organizations now affiliated with associations not recognized by the American Federation of Labor as bonafide labor organizations.

Submitted by:

Charles P. Howard,
Frank Dubinsky,
Frank B. Powers,
John J. Lewis,
A. A. Myrup,
J. C. Lewis.

[The minority report was defeated 18,024 to 10,933.]

III. Responses to Unionism

Given the nature of post-Civil War capitalism, it was hardly surprising that industry not only discouraged labor organizations but often fought them bitterly. In an age dedicated to the rapid accumulation of wealth, made possible in many cases by ruthless industrial competition, labor costs had to be kept to a minimum and production speeded up. To improve working conditions, raise wages, and reduce the length of the working day was to increase the costs of production, and a benevolent employer might well find that his less scrupulous colleagues had driven him from the competitive market. But employers did not have to rest their case on selfish grounds; they could appeal to certain allegedly fixed natural laws. Supply and demand, it was said, would determine the matter of wages and hours; moreover, the man who was dissatisfied with his working conditions could always exercise that fundamental American right to quit his job and find employment elsewhere.

But employers were by no means unanimous in their approach to organized labor. Some remained openly and immovably hostile; others approved of unions so long as they did not interfere with the inherent right of an employer to carry on his business as he saw fit, to hire and fire his employees, and to set the wages, hours, and working rules of his establishment—in other words, so long as they confined themselves to obtaining social benefits for their members and left economic questions to the employer and the laws of supply and demand; and still others, "enlightened" industrialists like Mark Hanna and his National Civic Federation, went so far as to recognize the value of collective bargaining with trade unions, especially those which patterned themselves after the conservative, business-minded American Federation of Labor. If worker unrest could be channeled into such an organization, then industry would most assuredly be safe from any major social upheaval or from more radical alternatives such as the I.W.W. By the 1920's, some employers hoped that scientific management and corporate paternalism would render even the A.F. of L. unnecessary, but the economic depression dashed such hopes and precipitated a new wave of industrial warfare.

Recognition of the legitimacy of trade-unions did not end the problems of capital and labor, but it did increase the possibility of a peaceful solution. By the mid-twentieth century, business and political leaders were not likely to object to the organization of labor, for this now had the sanction of the courts and the Federal government, but they did question the growing power of the unions, the revelations of deep-seated corruption in some labor organizations, and the allegedly diminishing rights of the nonunion worker, i.e., the worker who chose not to join a trade-union. Although some of these critics had simply found a more subtle means of checking the power of organized labor, the questions they raised were by no means unreal.

THE THREAT OF ALIEN IDEOLOGIES

Against a background of economic depression, the Railroad Strikes of 1877 presented industry and the public with the spectacle of America's first major labor uprising. That the strikes, which interrupted railroad traffic in a large part of the country, erupted almost spontaneously (the railroad brotherhoods having been reduced to fraternal lodges) made them that much more impressive. When militia detachments failed to restore railroad service and "law and order" (the Philadelphia militiamen were actually besieged in a roundhouse by a Pittsburgh crowd, infuriated at the killing of twenty-two of its citizens), President Rutherford B. Hayes ordered federal troops into action. In Baltimore, Pittsburgh, St. Louis, and Chicago, troops and strike sympathizers fought pitched battles in the streets, resulting in the death of over one hundred workers. At one point, *The New York Times* said of Chicago: THE CITY IN POSSESSION OF COMMUNISTS. All but forgotten were the issues that provoked the first outbreak at Martinsburg, West Virginia, on July 16—a reduction of wages, long hours, poor working conditions, and long hostility to any effective union organization. By August 1, the strikes had been broken, the workers' demands spurned, and railroad service restored. But the specter raised by the strikes could not be so easily dismissed. In the following selections, two influential molders of American opinion in the 1870's—E. L. Godkin's *The Nation* and the Rev. Henry Ward Beecher, silver-tongued pastor of the Plymouth Congregational Church of Brooklyn, New York, seek to assign responsibility.

The Nation (1877) *

It is impossible to deny that the events of the last fortnight constitute a great national disgrace, and have created a profound sensation through-

* From *The Nation,* XXV (August 2, 1877), pp. 68-69.

out the civilized world. They are likely to impress the foreign imagination far more than the outbreak of the Civil War, because the probability that the slavery controversy would end in civil war or the disruption of the Union had been long present to people's minds both at home and abroad. . . . There has for fifty years been throughout Christendom a growing faith that outside the area of slave-soil the United States had —of course with the help of great natural resources—solved the problem of enabling labor and capital to live together in political harmony, and that this was the one country in which there was no proletariat and no dangerous class, and in which the manners as well as legislation effectually prevented the formation of one. That the occurrences of the last fortnight will do, and have done, much to shake or destroy this faith, and that whatever weakens it weakens also the fondly cherished hopes of many millions about the future of the race, there is unhappily little question. We have had what appears a widespread rising, not against political oppression or unpopular government, but against society itself. What is most curious about it is that it has probably taken people here nearly as much by surprise as people in Europe. The optimism in which most Americans are carefully trained, and which the experience of life justi-fies to the industrious, energetic, and provident, combined with the long-settled political habit of considering riotous poor as the products of a monarchy and aristocracy, and impossible in the absence of "down-trodden masses," has concealed from most of the well-to-do and intelli-gent classes of the population the profound changes which have during the last thirty years been wrought in the composition and character of the population, especially in the great cities. Vast additions have been made to it within that period, to whom American political and social ideals appeal but faintly, if at all, and who carry in their very blood traditions which give universal suffrage an air of menace to many of the things which civilized men hold dear. So complete has the illusion been that up to the day of the outbreak at Martinsburg thousands, even of the most reflective class, were gradually ridding themselves of the belief that force would be much longer necessary, or, indeed, was now neces-sary in the work of government. . . .

The kindest thing which can be done for the great multitudes of un-taught men who have been received on these shores, and are daily ar-riving, and who are torn perhaps even more here than in Europe by wild desires and wilder dreams, is to show them promptly that society as here organized, on individual freedom of thought and action, is im-pregnable, and can be no more shaken than the order of nature. The most cruel thing is to let them suppose, even for one week, that if they had only chosen their time better, or had been better led or better armed, they would have succeeded in forcing it to capitulate. In what way better provision, in the shape of public force, should be made for its defense we have no space left to discuss, but that it will not do to be caught again as the rising at Martinsburg caught us; that it would be fatal to private and public credit and security to allow a state of things to subsist in which 8,000 or 9,000 day laborers of the lowest class can suspend, even for a whole day, the traffic and industry of a great nation, merely as a means of extorting ten or twenty cents a day more wages from their employers, we presume everybody now sees. Means of prompt and effectual prevention—so plainly effectual that it will never need to be resorted to—must be provided, either by an increase of the standing army or some change in the organization of the militia which will improve its discipline and increase its mobility. There are, of course, other means of protection against labor risings than physical ones, which ought not to be neglected, though we doubt if they can be made to produce much effect on the present generation. The exercise of greater watchfulness over their tongues by philanthropists, in devising schemes of social improvement, and in affecting to treat all things as open to discussion, and every question as having two sides, for purposes of legislation as well as for purposes of speculation, is one of them. Some of the talk about the laborer and his rights that we have listened to on the platform and in literature during the last fifteen years, and of the capacity even of the most grossly ignorant, such as the South Carolina fieldhand, to reason upon and even manage the interests of a great community, has been enough, considering the sort of ears on which it now falls, to reduce our great manufacturing districts to the condition of the Pennsylvania mining regions, and put our very civilization in peril. Persons of humane tendencies ought to remember that we live in a world of stern realities, and that the blessings we enjoy have not been showered upon us like the rain from heaven. Our superiority to the Ashantees or the Kurds is not due to right thinking or right feeling only, but to the determined fight which the more enlightened part of the community has waged from generation to generation against the ignorance and brutality, now of one class and now of another. In trying to carry on the race to better things nobody is wholly right or wise. In all controversies there are wrongs on both sides, but most certainly the presumptions in the labor controversy have always been in favor of the sober, orderly, industrious, and prudent, who work and accumulate and bequeath. It is they who brought mankind out of the woods and caves, and keep them out; and all discussion which places them in a position of either moral or mental inferiority to those who contrive not only to own nothing, but to separate themselves from property holders in feeling or interest, is mischievous as well as foolish, for it strikes a blow at the features of human character which raise man above the beasts.

Rev. Henry Ward Beecher (1877) *

Plymouth Church was crowded last evening by a large audience, and Mr. Beecher in the course of his discourse alluded to the great railroad strike. He said that disorder had broken out all along the great roads of several portions of the country, and riots of an unusual magnitude had taken place.

This Sabbath day was not, he said, one of stillness, for there were military movements throughout the land, and from their city soldiers were being dispatched to quell the riots. In a few days peace would be restored. Such outbreaks were but transient bubbles, which burst almost as soon as they were formed. They sprang from ignorance and passion. Such riots arose because their promoters and those who abetted them were ignorant of political economy. The question of labor and capital was a question of citizenship and of corporate life. He proceeded to eulogize the working classes, and dwelt particularly on the industry, sobriety, and heroism of the railroad employees, and pointed out the necessity for harmonious working together of the laborer and the capitalist. He explained at great length the elementary principles of political economy, and dwelt particularly on the causes which gave rise to the long depression of trade in this country. This portion of his discourse was a reproduction of his lecture on "Hard Times," and was frequently applauded. He then said: "What right had the working men, the members of those great organizations, to say to any one, 'You shall not work for wages which we refuse.' They had a perfect right to say to the employers, 'We shall not work for you,' but they had no right to tyrannize over their fellowmen. They had put themselves in an attitude of tyrannical opposition to all law and order and they could not be defended. The necessities of the great railroad companies demanded that there should be a reduction of wages. There must be continual shrinkage until things come back to the gold standard, and wages, as well as greenbacks, provisions and property, must share in it. It was true that $1 a day was not enough to support a man and five children, if a man would insist on smoking and drinking beer. Was not a dollar a day enough to buy bread? Water costs nothing. (Laughter.) Men cannot live by bread, it is true; but the man who cannot live on bread and water is not fit to live. (Laughter.) When a man is educated away from the power of self-denial, he is falsely educated. A family may live on good bread and

* From *The New York Times,* July 23, 1877.

water in the morning, water and bread at midday, and good water and bread at night. (Continued laughter.) Such may be called the bread of affliction, but it was fit that man should eat of the bread of affliction. Thousands would be very glad of a dollar a day, and it added to the sin of the men on strike for them to turn and say to those men, 'You can do so, but you shall not.' There might be special cases of hardship, but the great laws of political economy could not be set at defiance." He concluded by declaring that in the end, the men on strike would be defeated, trade resumed, and prosperity once more reign throughout the land. (Applause.).

. . . We look upon the importation of the communistic and like European notions as abominations. Their notions and theories that the Government should be paternal and take care of the welfare of its subjects and provide them with labor, is un-American. It is the form in which oppression has had its most disastrous scope in the world. The American doctrine is that it is the duty of the Government merely to protect the people while they are taking care of themselves—nothing more than that. "Hands off," we say to the Government; "see to it that we are protected in our rights and our individuality. No more than that." The theories of Europe in regard to the community of property we reject because they are against natural law and will never be practicable. God has intended the great to be great and the little to be little. No equalization process can ever take place until men are made equal as productive forces. It is a wild vision, not a practicable theory. The European theories of combinations between workmen and trade-unions and communes destroy the individuality of the person, and there is no possible way of preserving the liberty of the people except by the maintenance of individual liberty, intact from Government and intact from individual meddling. Persons have the right to work when or where they please, as long as they please, and for what they please, and any attempt to infringe on this right, and to put good workmen on a level with poor workmen—any such attempt to regiment labor is preposterous.

* From the Sermon of July 29, 1877, as reported in *The New York Times,* July 30, 1877.

CONTENTMENT OF THE WORKING CLASS

A Massachusetts Mill Owner (1883) *

When they [the workers] get starved down to it, then they will go to work at just what you can afford to pay. I remember going through 1840, 1841, and 1842. We had very hard times all through that period, and the manufacturers were losing money. . . . Mine was a small mill, but it will perhaps illustrate what others had to do as well as any illustration that I can give. I found that I could not run the mill and hold my own. I had not capital enough to run through and afford to lose anything. I sent to my help and asked them whether, if I could manage to run the mill through the winter they would be willing to work for less wages, and they said no. One man said he had a family of five or six children, and he said he would take his family to the poorhouse before he would work for less. I said very well, I would not run the mill. I shut it up and went home, myself and my wife, and stayed there through the winter with my father.

In the spring I went back and found that there people had been idle through the winter. I went into the mill building and lit a fire and the smoke began to curl up and go off through the chimney, and it was seen throughout the neighborhood, and they all came flocking to the mill to inquire if I were going to start. Among the others who came to make that inquiry was the man who said he wouldn't work for less than his own price. When he said, "Are you going to start?" I said, "I don't know." "For God's sake," he says, "start this mill, and give us just what you can afford to pay for our work." Said he, "I have had no work through the winter, except occasionally a job at chopping wood at 50 cents a cord, and I couldn't do more than one cord a day, and with that 50 cents I have got Indian meal to feed my family on." I said to him, "I told you last fall it would be hard for you, and you said you would rather go to the poorhouse." "Well," said he, "I was mistaken, and I am willing to go to work now." When help find that they cannot do any better, and learn that they have to go to work for a certain price or get nothing, they will go to work.

Q. Have you ever had strikes in your factories since 1865?
A. Yes.

* From the testimony of Charles L. Harding, President of the Merchants' Woolen Company, Dedham, Massachusetts, October 17, 1883. U.S. Congress, Senate, *Report of the Committee of the Senate upon the Relations between Labor and Capital* (Washington: U.S. Government Printing Office, 1885), III, 288-289, 293-294, 295.

Q. How many?

A. We had one, I think, in about 1873 or 1874. I never had but one strike in our mill.

Q. That was on account of a reduction of wages?

A. Yes. It was about the time they tried to strike for ten hours. The law was not then in existence to force us to go to ten hours. They struck for that, and for a little higher wages; but at the time business was very poor. We had been running at a loss for the six months previous, and had lost $50,000 in that time; but some of the advisers of our help advised them to turn out and strike for various things of that kind. I think the ten-hour rule was one thing they demanded; and another was more pay to certain proportions of them—weavers and spinners, I think. Then we let the mills stand as long as they wanted to, and when they got ready to go to work again on our terms we started up. I think that we stopped then about six weeks. The hands stood it until they could not get trusted any more at the stores, and some had been off to some other places to see if they could not do better, and had spent their money, and they wanted to go to work. Meanwhile, others had come in from abroad and wanted to go to work, so that there was no difficulty when we concluded to start again; we had plenty of help. We made no change. . . .

Q. Are your operatives generally healthy?

A. Very; there is very little sickness.

Q. They seem to be contented and satisfied generally, as a class?

A. There is no trouble; they are perfectly quiet and satisfied, unless some of these smart young men, that think they know more about it than the help do, undertake to come in sometimes and tell them they do not know what they are about; that they are a kind of slavish set working for exploiters, and ought to set up for independence, and start strikes, etc. However, our folks never tried that but once on us. I think they learned that it did not pay them.

A New Hampshire Mill Manager (1883) *

By Mr. PUGH:

Q. What is the general health of your employees?

A. I think that the general health may be said to be good. It is the

---

* From the testimony of Thomas L. Livermore, Manager of the Amoskeag Manufacturing Company, Manchester, New Hampshire, October 12, 1883. U.S. Congress, Senate, *Report of the Committee of the Senate upon the Relations between Labor and Capital* (Washington: U.S. Government Printing Office, 1885), III, 5-11, 13-15.

desire of the mill managers in this part of the country, generally, I believe, to light, heat, ventilate, and care for their mills generally so as to make them as healthy and agreeable as circumstances will allow; for other considerations not taken into account, the best mill in this respect would produce the best and the most cloth. Bad ventilation and discomfort generally has, I think, a palpable effect upon the quantity and character of product of the mill. The operative working in a well-lighted, well-heated, and well-ventilated mill would retain his strength and spirits to the end of the day, when one working in a mill which was not well-lighted and heated and ventilated, would flag toward the end of the day and not be at his best as a laborer.

HOURS OF MILL LABOR IN NEW HAMPSHIRE

The hours of labor in the mills here, for those who work the longest are from 6:30 a.m. to 12 and from 1 to 6:45 p.m. and on Saturday until 4 p.m.; making an average of about ten and three-quarter hours per day for each of the six working days of the week. But large numbers of the employees in the mill are enabled to finish their work sooner than the rest, and *they* average ten hours and some of them less per day.

OLD-TIME HOURS OF MILL LABOR

I am informed, and have no doubt from my investigation that it is true, that forty years ago the hours of labor averaged fourteen and a half per day in the mills; that they were gradually reduced by the voluntary act of the mill managers until they reached the limit which I have given as that of today. I suppose this reduction was made possible, and was in a large degree due to the improvements in machinery and methods of manufacture which enabled the mills to keep up their product as time went on with reduced hours of labor. . . .

CONTENTMENT OF MILL OPERATIVES
IN NEW HAMPSHIRE

By the Chairman
Q. What is your knowledge of the state of feeling among your operatives, as a general fact, as to their satisfaction with their condition, their living, and their wages, their contentment or discontent or distrust, or any want of confidence in their employers? We want to get at the relation and state of feeling in point of fact existing between the employers and employees.

A. I think that as a whole, the working people in our employ are not discontented with their pay or their condition. Of course, I suppose that every one on earth who is employed would be glad if he could get more wages than he does get, but I think that, generally, in this place, the people are contented to remain on the terms under which they are employed. . . .

NO LABOR UNIONS IN MANCHESTER, N.H.

Q. Have you any labor unions here? What is the fact as to the number of your employees who belong to labor unions?

A. I do not think that there is a labor union in this city, and I do not think that there has ever been one here which lasted. There have been several attempts to form unions since I have been here by agitators from the outside, mainly from Fall River, I think, and from one cause or another they have always failed.

STRIKES

Upon inquiry and investigation I have been led to believe that there has never been more than one general strike in this place, and that occurred about thirty years ago. I think that was a strike due to a change in the hours of labor, which was instituted by the mills, and I believe that the strike failed. Since that time there have been small strikes of detached portions of employees, but I never heard of one resulting in success. Some three or four years ago I had a strike of about one hundred of my dyers for higher wages. I thought that the strike was unreasonable and refused to accede to the demands of the strikers, and the result was that after staying away from their work about a week a large part of them—one half or more—came and asked me to take them back in the employ of the company. At that time I took pains to personally interrogate all of the men who came to me, to inquire why they had taken that means of trying to get higher wages, and I must say that with one or two exceptions they seemed to have been actuated rather by the fear of being odd and the fear of the censure of their fellow workmen than by any discontent of their situation. . . .

POWER OF ENDURANCE OF MILL OPERATIVES

Q. What is your observation as to the length of time or the hours of labor that the operative is capable of enduring without physical or other injury?

A. My belief is that he can work ten and three-quarter hours on an average without injury, and I may say that in a limited degree I had some experience myself as a youth, for I worked at a mechanical employment for a while; but of course my judgment must be formed mainly from my observation here. If one goes upon the main street here in the evening—Elm street—he will see the sidewalks crowded as densely as Broadway, New York, by the mill operatives who have finished their work and got their suppers and come out to promenade and see the shops and each other, and they seem to be merry and happy and laughing. I do not think that it is an exaggeration to say that you may often see on the sidewalks here in the evening thousands who have come out under those circumstances. Now, if it were the fact that they were prostrated and tired out by the hours of labor, they would not be out I think as a rule. . . .

Much of the work that is done by the day in the mills is such work as tending cards and the carding machinery, such as fly-frames, draw-frames, spinning-frames, etc., by women and girls. That is not labor requiring strenuous muscular exertion. They are sitting down much of the time, when a mill is running as we like to have it done. This labor requires attention. They must go to one frame or another and tie a piece of thread that is broken, or take off or put on a bobbin, or put on a spoon with "roving," and that is labor which does not require muscular exertion to any considerable extent, but requires attention. That machine never tires. It does as much in the eleventh hour as it does in the first hour. It is the machine that does the work; it is the operative who keeps her eye upon it and keeps it fed with material and keeps it cleared out of the manufactured article, . . . and I really do not think she can give any closer attention in the first hour than in the eleventh hour, provided she is a healthy person, fit to work in a mill. . . .

Q. Suppose a system were introduced of paying, substantially, by the hour or by the piece, and it prevailed all through your entire system of work, and then the proposition was made to the operatives to absolutely limit the hours of labor to ten, nine, or eight hours. Do you think that the operatives themselves would approve of that proposition, or would they prefer to work longer and get more pay?

A. I do not think they would approve of it. . . .

The Chairman. I asked the question because the suggestion has been made by many labor reformers, as they are termed, that even six hours, considering the increased productive power of machinery or of the human being and machinery combined, would be as long as laboring people ought to be expected to work—as long as the interests of society require that they should, and inasmuch as there are many unemployed people, a reduction of the hours of labor would give something to others to do. The question whether it could be made to work practically is the serious thing.

The Witness. I do not believe at all in such theories. I think that at least in a free country like this, with thousands of miles of land to be taken up in a vast area of country which is inhabited by people occupied in industrial pursuits, and the great variety of employments to be found in this country, it is perfectly safe for at least the lifetime of this generation to leave the question of how a man shall work, and how long he shall work, and where he shall work, and what wages he shall get, to himself. It is as certain that wages in a country situated as ours is, will adjust themselves to the level required by the demand and the market, as it is that water will seek its level. I do not believe that any one has ever yet seen in this country a time when distress on the part of the laboring people was universal. It has occurred in certain industries and in certain places without any question, but, every time, the tremendous field which is afforded to the laboring man in which to find employment has come to his relief, and with a little foresight, a little forehandedness, and a little energy, he has been able to find some employment in which he could earn his living and a little more. . . .

CHILD LABOR IN COTTON MILLS

Q. Won't you please tell us your experience with the question of child labor; how it is, and to what extent it exists here; why it exists, and whether, as it is actually existing here, it is a hardship on a child or on a parent; or whether there is any evil in that direction that should be remedied?

A. There is a certain class of labor in the mills which, to put it in very common phrase, consists mainly in running about the floor—where there is not as much muscular exercise required as a child would put forth in play, and a child can do it about as well as a grown person can do it—not quite as much of it, but somewhere near it, and with proper supervision of older people, the child serves the purpose. That has led to the employment of children in the mills, I think. . . .

Now, I think that when it is provided that a child shall go to school as long as it is profitable for a workman's child (who has got to be a workingman himself) to go to school, the limit has been reached at which labor in the mills should be forbidden. There is such a thing as too much education for working people sometimes. I do not mean to say by that that I discourage education to any person on earth, or that

I think that with good sense any amount of education can hurt any one, but I have seen cases where young people were spoiled for labor by being educated to a little too much refinement. . . .

THE PREROGATIVE AND RESPONSIBILITY OF THE EMPLOYER

In May 1894, workers of the Pullman Palace Car Co. went out on strike, protesting wage cuts, the discharge of men who had acted on the bargaining committee, and an accumulation of grievances. The American Railway Union, headed by Eugene Debs and organized along industrial rather than craft lines, agreed to support the strike and refused to handle Pullman cars. The result was an extensive railroad tie-up, some rioting in Chicago, the dispatch of federal troops by President Grover Cleveland (over the objections of the Illinois Governor), a court injunction, the breaking of the strike, and a subsequent government investigation. The testimony which follows is typical of the labor philosophy which prevailed in the Pullman Company and in many other industrial enterprises at this time.

Thomas H. Wickes (1894) *

Commissioner KERNAN. What is the basis of your objection to that union?

Answer. Our objection to that was that we would not treat with our men as members of the American Railway Union, and we would not treat with them as members of any union. We treat with them as individuals and as men.

Commissioner KERNAN. That is, each man as an individual, do you mean that?

Answer. Yes, sir.

Commissioner KERNAN. Don't you think, Mr. Wickes, that would give the corporation a very great advantage over these men if it could take them up one at a time and discuss the question with him. With the ability that you have got, for instance, where do you think the man would stand in such a discussion?

Answer. The man has got probably more ability than I have.

* From the testimony of Thomas H. Wickes, Second Vice-President of the Pullman Palace Car Company, August 27, 1894. U.S. Congress, House, United States Strike Commission, *Report on the Chicago Strike of June-July, 1894* (Washington: U.S. Government Printing Office, 1895), pp. 621-622.

Commissioner KERNAN. You think that it would be fair to your men for each one of them to come before you and take up the question of his grievances and attempt to maintain his end of the discussion, do you?

Answer. I think so; yes. If he is not able to do that that is his misfortune.

Commissioner KERNAN. Don't you think that the fact that you represent a vast concentration of capital, and are selected for that because of your ability to represent it, entitles him if he pleases to unite with all of the men of his craft and select the ablest one they have got to represent the cause?

Answer. As a union?

Commissioner KERNAN. As a union.

Answer. They have the right; yes, sir. We have the right to say whether we will receive them or not.

Commissioner KERNAN. Do you think you have any right to refuse to recognize that right in treating with the men?

Answer. Yes, sir; if we chose to.

Commissioner KERNAN. If you chose to. Is it your policy to do that?

Answer. Yes, sir.

Commissioner KERNAN. Then you think that you have the right to refuse to recognize a union of the men designed for the purpose of presenting, through the ablest of their members, to your company the grievances which all complain of or which any complain of?

Answer. That is the policy of the company; yes, sir. If we were to receive these men as representatives of the unions they could probably force us to pay any wages which they saw fit, and get the Pullman Company in the same shape that some of the railroads are by making concessions which ought not to be made.

Commissioner KERNAN. Don't you think that the opposite policy, to wit, that all your dealings with the men, as individuals, in case you were one who sought to abuse your power, might enable you to pay to the men, on the other hand, just what you saw fit?

Answer. Well, of course a man in an official position, if he is arbitrary and unfair, could work a great deal of injustice to the men; no doubt about that. But then it is a man's privilege to go to work somewhere else.

Commissioner KERNAN. Don't you recognize as to many men, after they had become settled in a place at work of that kind, that really that privilege does not amount to much?

Answer. We find that the best men usually come to the front; the best of our men don't give us any trouble with unions or anything else. It is only the inferior men—that is, the least competent—that give us the trouble as a general thing.

Commissioner KERNAN. As a rule, then, the least competent men make the most trouble, do they?

Answer. Yes, sir; if these gentlemen allow themselves to be led by the incompetent men that is their misfortune.

*   *   *

[That employers were not unanimous in their view of organized labor was made abundantly clear during the 1902 strike of the United Mine Workers in the Pennsylvania anthracite coal fields. Marcus A. Hanna, an industrialist and Ohio Senator, took the position of that "enlightened" class of employers who sought labor-capital cooperation for its obvious economic benefits and to keep labor from turning to more radical alternatives. The National Civic Federation, embodying representatives of industry, labor, and the public, popularized and hoped to implement this approach. During the coal strike, it appointed Hanna as chairman of a conciliation committee to bring the miners and operators together and help them resolve their differences. But George F. Baer, President of the Philadelphia and Reading Railroad Company (which also owned extensive mine properties), had little of Hanna's "enlightenment"; the negotiations broke down, Baer rejected the demands of the miners, ignored the advice of some of his industrial colleagues, and finally provoked the anger and intervention of President Theodore Roosevelt. The following selections briefly summarize the conflicting approach of these two industrial leaders to the questions of labor relations and employer responsibility. L. L.]

George F. Baer (1902) *

WILKESBARRE, PENN., Aug. 20.—W. F. Clark, a photographer of this city, recently addressed a letter to President Baer of the Philadelphia and Reading Railroad Company, appealing to him as a Christian to settle the miners' strike. The writer said if Christ was taken more into our business affairs there would be less trouble in the world, and that if Mr. Baer granted the strikers a slight concession they would gladly return to work and the President of the Philadelphia and Reading would have the blessing of God and the respect of the nation.

President BAER replied as follows:

"I see you are evidently biased in your religious views in favor of the right of the working man to control a business in which he has no other interest than to secure fair wages for the work he does. I beg of you not to be discouraged. The rights and interests of the laboring man will be

* The New York Times, August 21, 1902.

protected and cared for, not by the labor agitators, but by the Christian men to whom God in His infinite wisdom has given the control of the property interests of the country. Pray earnestly that the right may triumph, always remembering that the Lord God Omnipotent still reigns and that His reign is one of law and order, and not of violence and crime."

Marcus A. Hanna (1902) *

To have success in conciliation, or arbitration, there must be thorough and effective organization on both sides. The large aggregations of capital, feared at first by labor, may prove to be labor's best friend, in that, control of a trade being thus centralized, there is opportunity to establish friendly relations which shall make uniform conditions throughout the country, or large sections thereof, and reduce the basis of competition to the quality of the product rather than to the concessions forced trom labor. . . .

My experience has taught me, my friends, that the employer because of his position has the most to do, and it must be expected that the employers, at least in the beginning of this educational work, should go more than half way. They provide work, and are responsible for the conduct of business, and upon them rests the responsibility of seeing that the men receive their share of its benefits. We must rise to a higher level, where we can have a broader view of this question, where we can tear ourselves away from the prejudices which have heretofore stood between capital and labor.

I believe in organized labor, and I have for thirty years. I believe in it because it is a demonstrated fact that where the concerns and interests of labor are entrusted to able and honest leadership, it is much easier for those who represent the employers to come into close contact with the laborer, and, by dealing with fewer persons, to accomplish results quicker and better.

The trusts have come to stay. Organized labor and organized capital are but forward steps in the great industrial evolution that is taking place. We would just as soon think of going back to primitive methods of manufacturing as we would to primitive methods of doing business, and it is our duty, those of us who represent the employers, from this time on to make up our minds that this question is one that must be heard.

You are well aware that there has been a tendency in this country,

* From Marcus A. Hanna, "Industrial Conciliation and Arbitration," *The Annals of the American Academy of Political and Social Science,* XX (1902), 21, 24-26.

from the very nature of things, to what is called socialism. Everything that is American is primarily opposed to socialism. We talk about it and regret that these conditions exist, regret that there are extremists who are teaching the semi-ignorant classes labor theories, that proceed upon the principle that liberty is license. That is a condition which must be met. It is the duty of every American citizen to assume his responsibilities in this educational work, and to assist any organization which can correct these theories and these ideas. There is no question concerning these theories and these ideas. There is no question concerning our body politic today that should command deeper or more serious thought. There is nothing in the organization of society in this country that can afford to permit the growth of socialistic ideas. They are un-American and unnatural to us as a people.

In the beginning of this work I received great encouragement from an address which Samuel Gompers [President of the American Federation of Labor] made in Cooper Union Institute, in New York, about a year and a half ago, when he took the broad ground that in the interests of labor there was no room for the socialist or the anarchist, no room for men who undertook to disturb the principles of our society and government. When such words came from a man leading the largest labor organization in the world, a man of advanced thought and of honest intent, I knew that now is the time to strike, now is the time to proclaim to the American people that in the consideration of this question, which sooner or later must be forced upon us, we must consider what is for the best interest of society as well as for our material development.

LABOR RACKETEERING

When a Senate Committee conducted some intensive and well publicized hearings on labor corruption and racketeering in the 1950's, it was simply focusing national attention on practices long acknowledged and tolerated in the American labor movement. Among the first of the labor racketeers was Sam Parks, a union business agent in the New York building trades—an industry particularly susceptible to corruption because of its speculative and seasonal character. Working in close cooperation with certain construction firms, Parks helped them to eliminate their competitors, enriched himself, and secured wage increases for his workers. When arrested and tried on extortion charges in 1903, his union replied by voting him a $1,000 bonus and re-electing him to his office.

In the two selections that follow, the first deals with an employer's experience with labor graft, while the second seeks to define union racketeering in the context of modern economic life.

Charles Piez (1914) *

Commissioner WEINSTOCK. You were telling us of the experience you had in New York some years ago with Sam Parks in the saddle, and how, despite the fact that he was a crook and bribe taker, he was knowingly kept in the saddle by the unions, so that you found it impossible to do business under those circumstances.

Mr. PIEZ. He was convicted, as you remember, Mr. Weinstock. That is the reason I said he was a crook—because he was a convicted one.

Commissioner WEINSTOCK. Could he have been a bribe taker if there had been no bribe giver?

Mr. PIEZ. You can't have one without the other; but if a man puts a gun up against your head, what are you going to do?

Commissioner WEINSTOCK. I suppose I would cough up if there was nothing else possible.

Mr. PIEZ. That is exactly what you would do, and that is what any employer would do. I have got just that kind of spirit.

Commissioner WEINSTOCK. I am not thoroughly familiar with the history of Sam Parks; I simply have an imperfect recollection of the circumstances, but as near as I can recollect, he was in the saddle for quite a while.

Mr. PIEZ. Quite a long time.

Commissioner WEINSTOCK. Can you tell us about how long?

Mr. PIEZ. I would not venture. Perhaps six or seven years. I am not real certain. He had succeeded in getting a considerable wage increase for the men. That is one thing, of course, that helped him maintain himself in the saddle, and I presume the men felt whatever else he could get was simply a perquisite of the job.

Commissioner WEINSTOCK. I presume it is safe to say that practically all of the time he was there he was a crook?

Mr. PIEZ. He may not have started as one. Perhaps opportunity made him one.

Commissioner WEINSTOCK. If it is a fact he was a crook for a good

* From the testimony of Charles Piez, President of the Link Belt Company (manufacturer of conveying and riveting machinery), Chicago, July 21, 1914. U.S. Congress, Senate, *Final Report and Testimony Submitted to Congress by the Commission on Industrial Relations,* 64th Cong., 1st Sess., Senate Doc. 415 (Washington: U.S. Government Printing Office, 1916), IV, 3188.

deal of that time, did not the manufacturers who were held up as stated here have the amplest possible time to bring him to justice?

Mr. Piez. Very likely.

Commissioner Weinstock. Then, were not the employers to blame for not having brought him to justice?

Mr. Piez. Taking it from a theoretical, highly moral point of view, yes, sir; from a practical point of view, I am not so certain. The consequence of engaging with a man like Parks, if you are in the construction business in a market like New York—a man who holds absolutely in his power the entire labor situation in the field you are engaged in, I think it would make a man think twice before he would proceed against him.

Commissioner Weinstock. As I recollect the circumstance, Parks was bribed by certain employers to declare strikes against other certain employers.

Mr. Piez. That was the rumor at the time.

Commissioner Weinstock. That was proven at the time?

Mr. Piez. I understand that was the rumor at the time. I don't know what the proof was.

Commissioner Weinstock. If that is the fact, were not those employers who bribed Parks to declare a strike as much to blame as Parks?

Mr. Piez. Just as criminal, and ought to have gone to the penitentiary with him.

Commissioner Weinstock. Did they?

Mr. Piez. I didn't hear of any of them going.

Commissioner Weinstock. So that it was a sort of one-sided punishment?

Mr. Piez. Punishment usually is. . . .

Commissioner Weinstock. What steps do employers take to drive out of their ranks dishonest employers?

Mr. Piez. They are taking more and more. All of this question has been much better generalized in the last ten years or more. I don't know whether you are an employer or manufacturer or not, but I think the standard of morals is higher today in every line of business than it ever was before, and I think the associations have a very large field doing just that sort of thing. We are, of course, small fry, and Parks, of course, held up the little fellows as well as the big. We had no interest in declaring strikes on the other fellow; we were simply the victims. He made it impossible to do anything except bow to his wishes.

*Subcommittee on Labor Unions of the Committee
on Legislation, City Club of New York
(1937)* *

Racketeering exposed in connection with labor unions is in no sense peculiar to labor unions; it is part of a criminal pattern that has manifested itself in such diversified fields as prostitution, lottery and policy games, bail bonding, and in liquor traffic, both now and prior to repeal of the Eighteenth Amendment, as well as in legitimate forms of business activity. In each case the purpose is the unlawful extortion of tribute for the personal gain of a few individuals; in each case these individuals are found to be criminals who may be cloaked in the trappings of respectability but whose illegal activities are not confined to the labor racket.

One feature which is sometimes considered peculiar to labor racketeering is that the means employed may include practices not intrinsically illegal, namely, the threat of union sanctions such as strikes and picketing. But the threat of lawful action is made in connection with other types of extortion. For example, the blackmailer menaces his victim with the threat of making public what may be a completely true statement of facts, or of reporting to law enforcement officers the commission by his victim of a crime. And a similar technique is found in unfair trade practice such as tying contracts or block-booking in the motion picture industry, through which a purchaser, in order to obtain a desired article, is compelled at the same time to purchase an undesired article. In each case the means, intrinsically lawful, become unlawful only because of the element of extortion.

That the means employed by the labor racketeer may not be unlawful makes it all the more important that the problem be approached with circumspection and with appreciation of the fact that labor racketeering is but a symptom of a far larger problem. Otherwise, proper efforts tending to bring into disrepute the lawful means employed by labor racketeers for unlawful ends may also tend to discredit legitimate labor activity for legitimate ends. . . .

"Labor racketeering" consists in essence of the use of a labor union by racketeers to exact payments to the racketeers from the employer, from members of the union, or from both. The racketeer may himself be a union official or he may operate from without the union either through

* Subcommittee on Labor Unions of the Committee on Legislation, *Report on Certain Aspects of Labor Union Responsibility and Control* (New York: City Club of New York, 1937), pp. 7-9.

his agents or through the exercise of coercion upon intimidated union officers. The labor racketeer is often enabled to maintain his dominant position through cooperation, passive or even active, on the part of the employer, whose inertia to the existence of a racket may be partially explained by the fact that the cost of the racket is usually passed on to the consumer, or to another branch of the industry, rather than borne by the employer himself. A further explanation may be found in the fact that the employer may actually profit by the racket. Thus, the employer may find it profitable to make periodic payments to a union officer in order to avoid compliance with a union rule, such as payment for overtime, or a requirement that members of the union shall not work with, or on the products of, nonunion labor. Or the employer may believe that the improvement of working conditions which may follow upon effective collective bargaining will cost him more than the labor racket.

Again, the employer may take advantage of the racket to drive a competitor out of business or to maintain prices in connection with certain types of so-called trade associations. This type of trade association, in conjunction with which labor racketeering flourishes most effectively, is usually organized and maintained in a large city and in a demoralized industry in which legitimate employer organization is not possible or its advantages not appreciated. The initial purpose of the association, which in its more refined forms may escape the sanctions of the antitrust laws, is to obtain higher prices or to stabilize competitive conditions. Ultimately, the visible gains to the members of the association may be so costly or the temptation to attract business by price-cutting so strong that coercion becomes necessary to compel members to remain in the association or to compel competitors to join it. An effective instrument for such coercion is found in the labor racketeer, who directs threats of labor trouble against those who might otherwise be unwilling to join or maintain membership in the trade association itself but also in other branches of the trade or industry in which the association functions.

Variations in the labor racket occur under varying conditions but the fundamental technique remains the same; upon analysis most labor rackets are found to be surprisingly similar.

The labor racketeer sometimes obtains such power that he is able to create an unnecessary type of work from which he obtains income. For example, an indictment against racketeers in a local of the teamsters' union charges that these racketeers through their control of trucking forced upon the dairy industry a duplication in terminal operations, resulting in a $300,000 annual increase in handling costs.

Through his dominance of the industry, the racketeer may even set up an independent business servicing the industry, patronage of which is required of employers wishing to avoid labor trouble. An outstanding example is a case in New Jersey in which a racketeer compelled contractors to patronize his construction bonding business. Another instance is that of a racketeer in control of a motion picture operators' union who forced theater owners to purchase supplies from him.

While the membership of a union dominated by a racketeer may on the whole be better off by reason of improved conditions than in the absence of any union, the membership also suffers from labor racketeering. Exploitation of union members by the racketeer takes the form of the "sell out," most commonly in the form of agreements unduly favorable to the employer, the "kickback," through requiring union members to return part of their wages to the employer or to union officers, the exaction of excessive dues, discrimination in union privileges or in the distribution of work, waiver of union rules or contract provisions, payment of excessive salaries to union officials or diversion or embezzlement of union funds. The racketeer-controlled union may also be used as a device to combat legitimate union activity.

While the employer may in the first instance pay the cost of a racket, that cost, like the cost of any other antisocial activity, is ultimately borne by the public in the form of increased prices and industrial strife. Some employers, such as small retailers, may suffer through being unable to pass on the racket cost, but, as we have pointed out, employers may obtain benefits from the labor racket through the maintenance of the price level and the elimination of effective collective bargaining. It is an interesting commentary upon the relationship that sometimes exists between the employer and the labor racketeer that the head of an employers association in a notoriously racket-ridden industry is reported to have asked that one of the principal convicted defendants be paroled in his custody pending an appeal. And in the recent trial of restaurant racketeers, it was brought out that substantial contributions to their defense fund were made by restaurant owners. It is true that employer groups protest the labor racket, but such protests are chiefly in the form of proposals for curbing all unions, whether corrupt or not, and, moreover, often come from groups not affected by racketeering.

UNIONISM AND PERSONAL LIBERTY:
ARE THEY COMPATIBLE?

Dudley Taylor (1914) *

Commissioner O'CONNELL. Now, Mr. Taylor, I take it you have given considerable thought to the question of how the wageworkers ought to be organized. I take it you are not opposed to wageworkers organizing.

Mr. TAYLOR. Not at all.

Commissioner O'CONNELL. What would you consider to be a proper method and proper organization of labor?

Mr. TAYLOR. Of course, that is hard to say, but I do feel this, that a labor organization ought to be in a position to merit the confidence of the public and of employers, for that matter, and ought not to rely upon coercion. But what do we see? We see members of labor unions who do not dare to go to the meetings of their union and raise their voice in protest. We continually read in the newspapers of this city how some man has been assaulted and possibly kicked downstairs for presuming to say something in a labor union meeting. I have talked with the members of labor unions regarding violence and graft—good, decent, respectable fellows—and I have said, "Why don't you have a house cleaning; why don't you go down there and why don't you take some of your people down there and open up these things and find out and be decent?" You simply get a smile from those fellows if they have one in their system. They don't dare do it. They are coerced into the union; they are coerced to do as the union directs, and we see the evidence of it every day. Some trouble is experienced somewhere in this city; a man goes around and perhaps whistles, blows a tin whistle, or snaps his fingers and the men go on a strike. Why? The chances are they don't know anything about it; the chances are they are opposed to it, because for the time being it takes their living from them or a considerable part of their living, but they have no choice or option but to obey. If those men were not coerced; if they were in fear of violence that would not be the case.

I say that the labor unions as organized today, generally speaking, are thriving on coercion. It should not be so; it should be voluntary.

* From the testimony of Dudley Taylor, General Counsel for the Employers' Association of Chicago, July 22, 1914. U.S. Congress, Senate, *Final Report and Testimony Submitted to Congress by the Commission on Industrial Relations,* 64th Cong., 1st Sess., Senate Doc. 415 (Washington: U.S. Government Printing Office, 1916), IV, 3237-3238.

This matter of the closed-shop proposition ought to be a voluntary proposition. The employer ought to be able to look at the contract and look over the union—the officers of the union—judging something of the past history, and say, I will be a lot better off doing business with your union; I want it in my business, and enter into the closed-shop agreement voluntarily, if he wishes to do so, and not to be compelled and coerced to do it and have the members coerced and compelled to go into the union and stay in the union and do as the union officers say. That is, in my judgment, un-American and wrong.

Commissioner O'CONNELL. What construction do you put on open shops? What is an open shop?

Mr. TAYLOR. An open shop, I take it, is a shop in which a man can be employed irrespective of his affiliation with any labor union.

Commissioner O'CONNELL. You think that is so?

Mr. TAYLOR. I think it is so. . . .

Commissioner O'CONNELL. Do you think that is so in any of the large industrial plants?

Mr. TAYLOR. I do know many, Mr. O'Connell, where the open shop has been in operation for years without any discrimination at all.

Commissioner O'CONNELL. And they are still open shops?

Mr. TAYLOR. They are still open shops.

Commissioner O'CONNELL. In reality or in name; which is it? . . .

Mr. TAYLOR. In reality, and I know I think what you have in your mind, and I am perfectly frank in answering you, if I am right, and that is this: That an employer who has been conducting an open-shop proposition gets into some trouble; he is up against a pretty hard proposition; perhaps he has learned a lesson or thinks he has learned a lesson; from that time on perhaps he maintains what he calls an open shop, and, as a matter of fact, it is closed to the union. That is what you have in mind, isn't it? In other words, he won't have a union member if he knows it?

Commissioner O'CONNELL. I believe that exists.

Mr. TAYLOR. That condition arises and exists.

Clarence S. Darrow (1915) *

Commissioner O'CONNELL. One of these subjects that has been before this commission more or less, and at this hearing particularly—two or

* From the testimony of Clarence S. Darrow, labor and criminal lawyer, May 18, 1915. U.S. Congress, Senate, *Final Report and Testimony Submitted to Congress by the Commission on Industrial Relations,* 64th Cong., 1st Sess., Senate Doc. 415 (Washington: U.S. Government Printing Office, 1916), XI, 10805-10806.

three gentlemen have called it everything but a respectable name, and that is the so-called union shop, known by the employers as the open and closed shop and by the union as a union shop or a nonunion shop. The employers charge criminality of purpose, depriving the American citizen of his right to work and the American employer of his right to employ whoever he pleases and under whatever conditions he pleases, and all that. I know you have spoken and written on this subject, and I am sure the commission would be glad to know, and I would, your opinion of the so-called open shop. . . .

Mr. DARROW. Of course, there is a lot of nonsense talked about it. They talk about the inalienable right of a man to work; he has no such right; no one has a right to work, and the man who stands for the open shop does not care for anybody's rights to work, except the nonunion man, and they only care for him because they can use him. If a man has any constitutional right to work he ought to have some legal way of getting work. If the Constitution is going to guarantee the right to work, it ought to guarantee some place to work, and there is no such thing. A man can only work if there is a job; he can only work for a man who wants some man to work for him.

The workingman spends a good share of his waking moments in a shop. He does not need to invite a nonunion man into his house if he does not want to, and probably won't, and he is under no more obligation to work with him in a factory if he does not want to. If a Presbyterian does not want to work with a Catholic, he may be narrow and bigoted, but he does not have to. Of course, a union man has a direct reason for it; he believes and he understands and feels that the nonunion man is working against the interests of his class; that the only way a workingman can get anything is by collective bargaining, and by saying, "If you don't give us a raise, not only I will quit but we will all quit and tie up your business"; that is the only way he can do it. One man quitting out of 50,000 is nothing, or even ten men or one hundred men, but if they all quit, so they can do with the employer what the employer does with you, when he discharges you, then they can bargain and there is no other kind of bargaining but collective bargaining.

The nonunion man comes along and says, "I will take your place." He is not loyal to the union, and the union man regards him as a traitor to his class, and he won't work with him, and he has a perfect right to refuse to work with him.

There is no such thing as the open shop, really. There is a union shop and a nonunion shop. Everybody that believes in the open shop disbelieves in the union shop, whatever they say; and I do not say that unions are perfect, they are not. The people that work with them know that better than anybody else. They are just doing the best they can with the job they have, which is a hard one, and with the material they have, which is not perfect. In many instances they are brutal, and have to be, and it is generally like the law, and works individual hardship here and there, but it is one of the necessary things in the industrial world, and the fight is between those who believe in unions and those who disbelieve in them. Those who disbelieve in them say they believe in the open shop; but the open shop is simply a back door to put the union man out.

Finley Peter Dunne (1920) *

"What's all this that's in the papers about the open shop?" asked Mr. Hennessey.

"Why, don't ye know?" said Mr. Dooley. "Really, I'm surprized at yer ignorance, Hinnissey. What is th' open shop? Sure, 'tis where they kape the doors open to accommodate th' constant stream av' min comin' in t' take jobs cheaper than th' min what has th' jobs. 'Tis like this, Hinnissey: Suppose wan av these freeborn citizens is workin' in an open shop f'r th' princely wage av wan large iron dollar a day av tin hour. Along comes anither son-av-gun and he sez t' th' boss, "Oi think Oi could handle th' job nicely f'r ninety cints." "Sure," sez th' boss, and th' wan dollar man gets out into th' crool woruld t' exercise hiz inalienable roights as a freeborn American citizen an' scab on some other poor devil. An' so it goes on, Hinnissey. An' who gits th' benefit? Thrue, it saves th' boss money, but he don't care no more f'r money thin he does f'r his right eye. It's all principle wid him. He hates t' see men robbed av their indipindence. They must have their indipindence, regardless av anything else."

"But," said Mr. Hennessey, "those open-shop min ye menshun say they are f'r unions if properly conducted."

"Shure," said Mr. Dooley, "if properly conducted. An' there we are: an' how would they have them conducted? No strikes, no rules, no contracts, no scales, hardly iny wages, an' dam' few mimbers."

* Finley Peter Dunne, "Mr. Dooley on the Open Shop." Quoted in *Literary Digest, LXVII* (November 27, 1920), 19. Through the characters of Mr. Dooley, an Irish saloon keeper in Chicago, and Mr. Hennessey, the perennial customer, newspaperman Finley Peter Dunne made a reputation as a keen wit and social critic.

Walter P. Reuther v. Senator Barry Goldwater
(1953) *

The Chairman [H. Alexander Smith of New Jersey]. Your thesis, Mr. Reuther, . . . does say that if fifty-one percent vote for the closed shop and forty-nine percent vote against it, that forty-nine percent will be compelled to join if they are going to be able to earn a livelihood. That is the thing that troubles so many people.

Mr. REUTHER. Let me try to develop that, because 1 know this is an area in which a lot of people feel very sensitive about this whole question, the right to work, and so forth. . . .

We think, you see, that the union is an attempt to extend the democratic processes in the industrial community; that organized society is based upon the principle that within the framework of a given society the people who make up that society have to work out rules and regulations to govern the relationship of one to the other.

Collective bargaining through the union is an attempt to extend that principle into the industrial community. People have rights and privileges and obligations in the community as a whole, but within industry they had no rights in the past. Collective bargaining is an attempt to establish their rights as economic citizens within the industrial community.

Obviously, in order to do that, they have to work out rules and regulations. They have to have the machinery of self-government. The union represents that kind of machinery.

The union performs some very important and essential functions. We handle grievances. We handle the grievances of all the workers. We have umpire machinery. The unions pay for the umpire machinery. When he hands down a decision, all the workers get the benefits. We have legal services. All the workers get the benefit of the cases we may process in unemployment compensation. All the workers get the benefit because we establish precedents; we work out basic policies. We have a medical department. We work on health problems. We work on occupational diseases. All the workers get the benefit of these.

Since all the workers in the industrial community get the benefits of these services performed by the union, made possible by the union, we believe that since all the workers share in the services all the workers ought to share in the cost of providing those services. . . .

The Chairman. It seems to me what you are arguing for is definitely

* From the testimony of Walter P. Reuther, President of the Congress of Industrial Organizations and the United Automobile Workers (UAW-CIO), cross-examined by Senator Barry Goldwater of Arizona, March 30, 1953. U.S. Congress, Senate, Committee on Labor and Public Welfare, *Hearings, Taft-Hartly Act Revisions*, 83d Cong., 1st Sess., 1953, Part 1, pp. 409-410, 415-417.

a government within the government. If you are going to set up a government within the government, we are going to be compelled to police certain internal affairs of the unions.

Mr. REUTHER. It is government by majority rule, and what is wrong with that? We fought the Revolutionary War around a very fundamental principle, and we were right: Around the idea of taxation without representation.

This is the other side of that coin. This is the matter of representation without taxation. One principle is as sound as the other, because if it is wrong to be taxed without representation, it is wrong to have representation without taxation.

Since all the workers in the industrial community have a right to vote democratically in determining whether our union is going to be the bargaining agency, we cannot get sole bargaining rights unless a majority of the workers support us at the National Labor Relations Board. So having gotten majority support, we then represent the machinery by which the workers in the industrial community govern themselves and have their work done. They all get the benefits of that machinery; they ought all to pay the taxes which make that machinery possible.

That is all we are asking. It seems to me that is a very sound thing.

The only test ought to be: No. 1, Is the government within the industrial community, represented by the union, established by democratic majority decision? No. 2, Is its membership open to all the people who have a right to participate in that industrial government? . . .

Senator GOLDWATER. Mr. Chairman.

I am very much interested in Mr. Reuther's development of the closed shop and the union shop. There is only one question in this whole field in my mind. What about the man who just does not want to belong to a union?

Mr. REUTHER. Well, if a fellow works in a General Motors plant and does not want to belong to a union, he does not have to work there.

Senator GOLDWATER. But suppose he wants to work there?

Mr. REUTHER. If you want to live in a certain community and you want the benefits of the work of that community, you have to pay taxes in that community. If you do not, you do not have to live in that community. That is the freedom of choice. The only check is that it has to be a democratic choice, decision; it has to be a majority democratic decision.

Inside of the industrial community, General Motors has 400,000 employees. How can a complex industrial society like ours work out machinery within this industrial community to meet these problems unless it can be done by a democratic decision of the people involved?

Senator GOLDWATER. I get down to the individual who does not want to belong to a union. Let us extend your thinking a little bit further. Take the matter of churches. Certainly churches benefit everybody. Yet we all do not support churches. Should we include laws to tax everybody to support churches in the community? Whether all of us agree or not, organizations like the Chamber of Commerce, for instance, do a lot of good for the people who live in the community, but I do not have to belong to the Chamber of Commerce and neither do you. Yet, because I am a member and pay my dues, I feel pretty much like you, as a union man, feel about the man who will not join your union, but I recognize the right of that competitor of mine or any other friend to say "yes" or "no" to membership in an organization that he will admit benefits him.

It gets down to that, and that is, in my mind, the only question: What about the individual?

Mr. REUTHER. The UAW-CIO, for example, to use a specific case, are certified as the sole collective bargaining agent. We represent every General Motors worker in our units. No church represents all the people in the community. You are dealing with an entirely different kind of thing. The church is a fraternal religious organization that you can choose to belong to or choose not to belong to; but our unions are the sole bargaining agent under the law. We represent every General Motors Worker. When we process a grievance, every General Motors worker gets the benefit of that. If we have a case that goes to the court on some workmen's compensation case, that sets a principle, and every GM worker gets the benefit of that protection that we want. If we have our doctors go in and check on the dust in a foundry or the fumes in a factory plant and we take corrective steps to protect the health of the workers, every worker in that plant gets the benefit of that.

The church does not perform that kind of function in the community. The church deals with the spiritual values. You can either choose to get them or you can choose not to get them.

But we are by law the agency by which all workers in a given factory take care of their industrial problems. In other words, we really are like a government within that factory, within that industrial community. If you are going to have a government within the industrial community, you have a right to insist that it is a democratic government; you have a right to insist that the workers who make up the industrial citizens in that industrial community have a right to elect their officers democratically, have a right to make democratic majority decisions. But having made the democratic majority decisions, the people in the minority are obligated to go along with the majority just as they are when you vote taxes for schools in your community. What is the difference? It is the same principle.

Senator GOLDWATER. I do not agree with you there. I see what you are getting at, and I think we could probably spend a whole year arguing about that point.

I keep getting back to the one question: Suppose a man does not want to belong to a union? You are not a government. The dues to the union cannot be compared to taxes. They do not bring all the benefits that taxes bring. I merely inject that.

Mr. REUTHER. They do in the industrial community.

Senator GOLDWATER. I wanted to get your thinking on what about the individual, because it all gets down, as you say, to the freedom of the individual, his desire to belong to a union or not, his desire to—let us forget churches—his desire to belong to the Chamber of Commerce or not, or to any other organization that might be helpful, to support the Red Cross or not, the Community Chest or not.

Mr. REUTHER. You go out to the Ford plant. I worked for six years in the Ford plant under the old system before we had a union. You talk to the workers out there. When they voted 88,000 to 1,000, that was an expression that they had found a new freedom. The union has given them greater freedom than we ever had, freedom from terror, and intimidation, and insecurity.

Senator GOLDWATER. I do not disagree with you. I agree with you. I think the unions have done wonderfully. But there are still a thousand men who do not want to belong to the union. You see what I am getting at. To my mind, you are tampering with the basic freedom that this Government is set up to give the people.

IV. The Weapons
of Resistance

Opponents of trade-unionism did not confine themselves to theoretical arguments. Had they done so, much of the violence that characterized labor-capital relations might have been averted. Those who chose to resist organization employed an assortment of weapons, ranging from the "yellow dog contract" and the blacklist to what the National Labor Relations Board defined in the 1930's as the Mohawk Valley Formula. The effectiveness of these various methods of opposition depended on the extent to which they were used, the strength of the union against which they were directed, and the attitude of the courts and the state and federal government.

Perhaps the glare of publicity in the 1930's did more than anything else to curtail the use of several of these weapons. Against a background of growing labor turbulence and C.I.O. attacks on the mass industries, a congressional committee headed by Senator Robert LaFollette, Jr., of Wisconsin uncovered and made public the often sordid details of employer opposition to unionization. By the 1940's partly as a result of this investigation, many of these antiunion devices had been outlawed or discredited, and a growing number of employers either turned to more subtle methods or decided upon union recognition and collective bargaining.

But even respectability, legislation, and more sympathetic courts did not immunize the labor organizer from harassment and attack. This was made abundantly evident, for example, in a 1951 congressional investigation of the Southern textile industry, where it was found that the labor organizer was subjected to constant surveillance, community antilabor groups, espionage, violence, injunctions, endless court litigation, and, if himself a worker in the mills, the loss of his job. If the organizer still managed to establish a union, the committee found that

the employers then go to work to bust the union; the grievance procedure is broken down; the disgruntled workers are urged by management to revoke the check-off of dues; union representatives are denied access to the plant; union leaders are fired. This may be called the softening-up process. When the contract comes up for renegotiation, impossible demands are made; negotiations drag on interminably; employees are propagandized on the unreasonable attitude of union negotiators; expiration of the contract forces a strike; injunction is secured; strikers are hailed for contempt; a back-to-work movement is started; fights are precipitated; workers are evicted from homes in the mill village; peace officers harass the strikers; the National Guard is called out; loans to union members are called in; credit is stopped; ministers urge return to work; the strike collapses under this conjunction of economic, physical, moral and religious pressure; returning employees are refused employment; blacklists block employment in other mills. If the strike cannot be broken, the plant can be closed and machinery transferred to another mill or sold.

Just as employers failed to agree on the wisdom of combating unionism, so they disagreed on the weapons to be employed. Some never used any of the devices described in this section; others may have abandoned them after several years; and still others may have preferred more subtle means. But the methods of resistance described here were by no means negligible in their effect; they successfully thwarted union organization in many industries and, wherever used, left a long heritage of hate and suspicion. They serve as a useful reminder of the often tortuous path unionization had to take.

THE "YELLOW-DOG" CONTRACT

Western Union Telegraph Co. (1883) *

I, ... of .... in consideration of my present reemployment by the Western Union Telegraph Co. hereby promise and agree to and with the said company that I will forthwith abandon any and all membership, connection or affiliation with any organization or society, whether secret or open, which in anywise attempts to regulate the conditions of my services or the payment thereof while in the employment now undertaken. I hereby further agree that I will, while in the employ of said company, render good and faithful service to the best of my ability, and will not in anywise renew or re-enter upon any relations or membership whatsoever in or with any such organizations or society.

Dated .... 1883. Signed .... Address .... (Seal)
Accepted for the Western Union Telegraph Co. ...., Superintendent

* From New York, *Third Annual Report of the Bureau of Statistics of Labor of the State of New York, for the Year 1885* (Albany, 1886), pp. 586-587.

Hitchman Coal & Coke Co. v. Mitchell (1917) *

About the 1st of June a self-appointed committee of employees called upon plaintiff's president, stated in substance that they could not remain longer on strike because they were not receiving benefits from the Union, and asked upon what terms they could return to work. They were told that they could come back, but not as members of the United Mine Workers of America; that thenceforward the mine would be run non-union, and the company would deal with each man individually. They assented to this, and returned to work on a nonunion basis. Mr. Pickett, the mine superintendent, had charge of employing the men, then and afterwards, and to each one who applied for employment he explained the conditions, which were that while the company paid the wages demanded by the Union and as much as anybody else, the mine was run nonunion and would continue so to run; that the company would not recognize the United Mine Workers of America; that if any man wanted to become a member of that union he was at liberty to do so; but he could not be a member of it and remain in the employ of the Hitchman Company; that if he worked for the company he would have to work as a nonunion man. To this each man employed gave his assent, understanding that while he worked for the company he must keep out of the Union.

Since January, 1908 (after the commencement of the suit), in addition to having this verbal understanding, each man has been required to sign an employment card expressing in substance the same terms. This has neither enlarged nor diminished plaintiff's rights, the agreement not being such as is required by law to be in writing. . . .

That the plaintiff was acting within its lawful rights in employing its men only upon terms of continuing nonmembership in the United Mine Workers of America is not open to question. Plaintiff's repeated costly experiences of strikes and other interferences while attempting to "run union" were a sufficient explanation of its resolve to run "nonunion," if any were needed. But neither explanation nor justification is needed. Whatever may be the advantages of "collective bargaining," it is not bargaining at all, in any just sense, unless it is voluntary on both sides. The same liberty which enables men to form unions, and through the union to enter into agreements with employers willing to agree, entitles other men to remain independent of the union and other employers to agree with them to employ no man who owes any allegiance or obligation

* From *Hitchman Coal & Coke Co.* v. *Mitchell,* 245 U.S. 239-240, 250-251, 259 (1917).

to the union. In the latter case, as in the former, the parties are entitled to be protected by the law in the enjoyment of the benefits of any lawful agreement they may make. This court repeatedly has held that the employer is as free to make nonmembership in a union a condition of employment, as the working man is free to join the union, and that this is a part of the constitutional rights of personal liberty and private property, not to be taken away even by legislation, unless through some proper exercise of the paramount police power. . . .

Upon all the facts, we are constrained to hold that the purpose entertained by defendants to bring about a strike at plaintiff's mine in order to compel plaintiff, through fear of financial loss, to consent to the unionization of the mine as the lesser evil, was an unlawful purpose, and that the methods resorted to by Hughes [Union organizer]—the inducing of employees to unite with the union in an effort to subvert the system of employment at the mine by concerted breaches of the contracts of employment known to be in force there, not to mention misrepresentation, deceptive statements, and threats of pecuniary loss communicated by Hughes to the men—were unlawful and malicious methods, and not to be justified as a fair exercise of the right to increase the membership of the union.

THE BLACKLIST

Iron Founders' and Machine Builders' Association of the Falls of the Ohio (1863) *

4th. Should the employees in any of our establishments stop work in order to force their employers to submit to unreasonable demands, the members of the "Iron Founders' and Machine Builders' Association of the Falls of the Ohio," and the members of the associations of other cities, or the establishments who have agreed to act in concert with these associations, shall not employ any men engaged in such strike. The names of the parties engaged in any attempt to force their employers to submit to unreasonable demands shall be sent in a circular at the expense of this Association to all the other associations or establishments with which we are in correspondence, in order that they may be prevented from getting employment until they either withdraw from the "Moulders'

* From the Address of the Iron Founders' and Machine Builders' Association of the Falls of the Ohio, September 3, 1863. Reprinted in *Fincher's Trades' Review*, October 3, 1863.

Union," or cease to attempt the enforcing of their unjust demands. Similar circulars received from the associations or establishments in other cities shall be respected by this Association in like manner.

A Telegraph Operator (1883) *

Q. Have you known any instances where men have made themselves conspicuous in asking for an increase of compensation and where they have been discriminated against on that account?

A. Yes, sir; anything in the shape of getting up petitions of that kind has resulted disastrously to the ringleaders.

Q. How do you mean disastrously? Have they been dismissed from the service, or have they been discriminated against while in the service?

A. Yes, sir; they have been either dismissed from the service or discriminated against in many ways. For instance, their chances for promotion would be greatly lessened; they would be looked upon as "agitators."

Q. Is there any difficulty in men discharged for such reasons obtaining employment elsewhere?

A. Yes, sir; their names are placed on the blacklist and managers all over the country are notified of it.

Q. How do you know that?

A. When they apply for situations the managers tell them that they are on the blacklist. For instance, a man applies for a situation in Philadelphia, and if he is obnoxious in that respect the manager in New York will telegraph back to the manager in Philadelphia that that man is not a proper person to employ. . . .

Q. Now, do you mean to say that a man would be placed on the blacklist and discriminated against, he being a good and skilled operator, only because he wanted more pay?

A. They give other reasons, other pretexts, of course, than the fact that a man has asked for an increase of wages or has instigated applications of that kind—they give other reasons; but it is a well-known fact, and it is the general belief of the operators that there is a system of blacklisting operators for entering into movements of that kind. . . .

Q. It is pretty well understood among the operators that a man who

* From the testimony of John Campbell, August 13, 1883, a telegraph operator and member of the Brotherhood of Telegraphers (affiliated with the Knight of Labor). U.S. Congress, Senate, *Report of the Committee of the Senate upon the Relations between Labor and Capital* (Washington: U.S. Government Printing Office, 1885), I, 113-114.

makes himself active in getting up an agitation for increase of pay occupies a dangerous position with reference to the company?

A. It is.

Q. Then there is a reluctance to do anything of that kind, I suppose?

A. Yes, sir; there has been such a feeling. Since the strike of 1870 various movements have been set on foot for the organization of the operators, but nearly all of them have fallen through because of intimidation by the officials of the company, particularly the local officials.

THE INJUNCTION

U.S. Industrial Commission (1902) *

. . . One of the most conspicuous features of the action of the courts in labor cases has been the injunction. The injunction is an order issued by a court under its equity power commanding certain persons to refrain from doing certain specified acts. Such orders are issued with a view to protect the rights and interests of individuals, or in some cases of the public, from threatened injury. Violation of an injunction constitutes contempt of court, and may be punished by the court itself with fine or imprisonment and without trial by jury.

There can be no doubt that the injunction has been much more extensively used in labor disputes by the American courts during the past ten years than ever before, and much more commonly in this country than in Great Britain. Both state and federal courts have restrained by injunction a large variety of acts. Public attention was generally called to the injunctions issued in connection with the great railroad strike of 1894; among them that which became the basis for the trial of E. V. Debs was especially far-reaching. It applied not only to the persons named as defendants, but also to "all other persons whatsoever who are not named herein, from and after the time when they shall severally have knowledge of such order." It prohibited interference with the business of a large number of the most important railroads of the country, or with trains engaged in interstate commerce or carrying the mails. It prohibited all persons from compelling or inducing by threats, persuasion, or intimidation, any of the employees of the railroads to refuse to perform their duties or to quit employment, and prohibited, almost as broadly,

* U.S. Congress, House, *Final Report of the Industrial Commission,* 56th Cong., 2d Sess., House Doc. 495 (Washington: U.S. Government Printing Office, 1902), XIX, 885-886.

efforts to prevent persons from entering employment. Numerous specific acts of violence and interference with property were also named. Finally, the order prohibited the doing of any act in furtherance of a conspiracy to prevent the operation of the railroads, or the directing or assisting of any person to commit any of the acts named. Many other injunctions have gone quite as far. Often they have specifically prohibited boycotts, picketing, and in one or two cases even the paying of strike benefits by labor unions. Some of the injunctions issued by lower courts have been modified by higher courts and made less far-reaching. In general, however, the courts have upheld injunctions against almost any act of workingmen which would constitute a ground for action for civil damages, or almost any act which might be the subject of criminal prosecution.

*   *   *

[Unable to break the Pullman strike of 1894 by any other means, including the intervention of federal troops, the employers and the federal government turned to the courts and secured a sweeping injunction, forbidding the workers to engage in virtually any action that might hamper the business of twenty-three specified railroads. Since compliance would have abruptly terminated the strike, the A.R.U. maintained its boycott of Pullman cars. In the following selection, Debs describes the impact of the injunction on the strikers. On May 27, 1895 the Supreme Court unanimously upheld the conviction of Debs and his associates for contempt of court. L.L.]

Eugene V. Debs (1894) *

. . . On the second day of July, I [Eugene Debs] was served with a very sweeping injunction that restrained me, as president of the union, from sending out any telegram or any letter or issuing any order that would have the effect of inducing or persuading men to withdraw from the service of the company, or that would in any manner whatsoever, according to the language of the injunction, interfere with the operation. . . . That injunction was served simultaneously, or practically so, by all of the courts embracing or having jurisdiction in the territory in which the trouble existed. From Michigan to California there seemed to be concerted action on the part of the courts in restraining us from exercising any of the functions of our offices. That resulted practically

* From the testimony of Eugene V. Debs, President of the American Railway Union, August 20, 1894. U.S. Congress, House, United States Strike Commission, *Report on the Chicago Strike of June-July, 1894* (Washington: U.S. Government Printing Office, 1895), pp. 142-144.

in the demoralization of our ranks. Not only this, but we were organized in a way that this was the center, of course, of operations. It is understood that a strike is war; not necessarily a war of blood and bullets, but a war in the sense that it is a conflict between two contending interests or classes of interests. There is more or less strategy resorted to in war, and this was the center in our operations. Orders were issued from here, questions were answered, and our men were kept in line from here.

At the time I was served with this injunction all of the officers at all of the points at the headquarters or terminals of all of these roads were served with a similar injunction restraining them all from sending any telegrams or from discharging the functions attached to their several offices. Following the issuance of that injunction a few days, I have forgotten the exact date, a special grand jury was convened for the purpose of examining into my conduct as president of the American Railway Union in connection with this trouble. The grand jury was in session very briefly, but found a bill upon an information that was filed, and I was ordered to be arrested. A warrant was issued and placed in the hands of a United States marshal for that purpose. On the 7th day of July, if I am not mistaken, I was arrested and brought before the court, and my bond was fixed, with my three official associates, Mr. Howard, vice-president; Mr. Rodgers, auditor of the Times, and Mr. Keliher, our secretary, we were simultaneously arrested and we were placed under a joint bond of $10,000. Very shortly after this there was an attachment issued for an alleged contempt of court, upon information that I had, as president, violated the injunction issued by Judges Wood and Grosscup.

Commissioner WRIGHT. That is, the injunction served on you on the second day of July?

Answer. Yes. As soon as the employees found that we were arrested and taken from the scene of action, they became demoralized, and that ended the strike. It was not the soldiers that ended the strike; it was not the old brotherhoods that ended the strike; it was simply the United States courts that ended the strike. Our men were in a position that never would have been shaken under any circumstances if we had been permitted to remain upon the field, remain among them; but once that we were taken from the scene of action and restrained from sending telegrams or issuing the orders necessary, or answering questions; when the minions of the corporations would be put to work at such a place, for instance, as Nickerson, Kansas, where they would go and say to the men that the men at Newton had gone back to work, and Nickerson would wire me to ask if that were true; no answer would come to the message, because I was under arrest, and we were all under arrest. The headquarters were demoralized and abandoned, and we could not answer any telegrams or questions that would come in. Our headquarters were temporarily demoralized and abandoned, and we could not answer any messages. The men went back to work, and the ranks were broken, and the strike was broken up by the Federal courts of the United States, and not by the Army, and not by any other power, but simply and solely by the action of the United States courts in restraining us from discharging our duties as officers and representatives of the employees. . . .

THE COMPANY UNION

John L. Lewis (1934) *

I do not know why a corporation thinks it has the right to organize, administer, regulate, operate, conduct, and finance a labor union of its employees. From the sheer standpoint of ethics I do not know why the United States Steel Corporation or the automobile industry, or any other industry would say to itself, "We will prevent our workers from having the kind of an organization which they desire to represent them, and we will prevent them from employing the kind of agents, the type of agents that they desire to represent them, and we will so arrange it that they can only have the kind of an organization that we wish to give them and they can only employ the type and character of an individual to represent them which is pleasing to us." . . .

I wish the Senators could have sat in on the hearings held this week in Washington before the National Labor Board on the conditions in the automobile industry. It was developed there from evidence that in the automobile industry in Detroit and other cities since the enactment of the Recovery Act, to which, in August and September of 1933, the automobile industry did by coercion and by intimidation form company unions; that the automobile industry did discriminate against numerous individuals and discharge them and deprive them of their employment, some of them after many years of service, for joining other unions than company unions and for talking of joining other unions than the company unions; that it did discharge certain of the elected representatives by company unions, elected in their shop unions, after those men found through experience that the company unions were but hollow mockeries and did join other unions; that the automobile industry, since the organization of the company unions, did deny the rights of collective bargaining

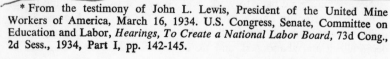

* From the testimony of John L. Lewis, President of the United Mine Workers of America, March 16, 1934. U.S. Congress, Senate, Committee on Education and Labor, *Hearings, To Create a National Labor Board,* 73d Cong., 2d Sess., 1934, Part I, pp. 142–145.

to workers who had organized themselves into other groups and other unions by refusing to meet them in conference except under such conditions, such stipulations that they found they could not accede to, for instance, turning over the list of their membership to the company without any guaranty that their members would not be discriminated against or discharged.

What was the formula for organizing the company unions in one of the plants of the General Motors? On a certain day the foreman of the shop, or a shop foreman, would go to the men of strong character in his shop, men of personality, with some elements of leadership, and tell them they were called at a meeting in the office that afternoon. The meeting would assemble that afternoon in the company office and they would be addressed by a representative of the company; they would be told that the company wanted to form a company union, that the company expected these people to help them, that these men would be paid their regular hourly rates for such help by the company. They were then given copies of the constitution and bylaws of such company union; they were told that an election would be held, that the company would fix the date of an election, that the company would supervise the election, that the election would be held in the plant, that ballot boxes would be provided, that the watchers would be designated, and they were asked to help, and they were asked under such conditions and under such circumstances that they testified that their refusal to participate or their refusal to help would in their judgment have jeopardized their standing with the company, and their jobs.

The arrangements were thus made; the notices of the election were posted; each individual in the shop was canvassed by his foreman or his subforeman; and each of them was told that the foreman desired to have a hundred percent record in his shop and he insisted that he go and vote and that the act of voting in the company-held election would make them members in good standing of this newly formed company union. They had no investment in it; they had no duty in the matter to perform except the dropping of a ballot in the box under the eye of the foreman or shop representative, and that made them members in good standing of this form of company union.

Witnesses testified that they resisted voting, that they were opposed to such participation, that they explained to the foreman they did not believe in that form of union, but they were asked to vote anyhow, and, against their will, they voted, and the returns were published that so many thousand men in this shop and this plant participated in the election and that they elected such representatives as were designated. The company fixed the requirements of representatives to be elected. It designated how many should be elected, or regulated the election and threw all manner of restrictions around it, and, in addition to that, the company financed it. They paid for the printing; they paid for the time of those key men in forming the organization; and it was testified that they pay the regular hourly rates to all of the representatives of this union in carrying out the business of the union and in taking up the grievances of individuals that arise in the ordinary course of its operation.

In other words, the company unions in the automobile industry are merely subsidiary organizations to the General Motors and other corporations engaged in that industry. They are subsidiary organizations just as much as a subsidiary sales company in another city. They are subsidiary organizations just as much as a captive coal company operating a captive mine for the Wheeling Steel Co. is to that company, and yet they seek to impose upon the workers this form of economic repression and they seek to chide those who would undertake to change that condition in this modern year of 1934.

FINKS, OPS, HOOKERS, AND THE HOOKED

Glossary (1938) *

Fink .... One who makes a career of taking employment in struck plants or of acting as a strikebreaker, strike guard, or slugger.

General Op .... A labor spy who holds an influential position in a labor union and reports on labor conditions in an entire city or area. . . .

Guard .... A fink serving on guard duty during a strike. Often armed.

Hooking .... Entrapping an employee into spying on fellow employees. Usually accomplished by approaching the prospective hooked man under a pretext and engaging him to write reports.

Hooker .... Detective agency official who induces workers to become spies.

Hooked man .... An employee engaged in industrial espionage without knowledge that he is report-

* U.S. Congress, Senate, Committee on Education and Labor, *Violations of Free Speech and Rights of Labor*, Senate Report 46, Part 3, 75th Cong., 2d Sess., 1938.

ing to a detective agency or that his reports are going to the employer. . . .

Inside man ....A spy placed in a plant as an employee. *See* Hooked man, Missionary, Outside man. . . .

Missionary ....A spy whose work it is to spread antiunion or antistrike propaganda in the general neighborhood of a plant and particularly among the wives of workers. One not employed in the plant.

Noble ....A lieutenant of strike operations usually in charge of a detachment of guards, sluggers, and finks.

Op ....*See* Operative.

Operative ....A spy employed by an agency. Usually has a secret designation. An operative may be a hooked man or professional spy.

Outside man ....A spy under a cover but not masquerading as an employee in a plant. *See* Missionary. . . .

Roping ....Securing information by striking up acquaintance or friendship with union men.

Rough shadowing ....To keep a man under surveillance in such a manner that he knows that he is being followed and is intimidated. . . .

Slugger ....A specialized type of fink used to attack, assault, and beat up strikers or union leaders. Generally armed. *See* Fink Guard.

Strikebreaker ....One whose trade it is to take employment in struck plants. Distinguishable from "scab" who is a workman. May pretend to work in the plant or act as a guard. A fink.

Soliciting Work (1917 and 1920) *

O'NEIL SECRET SERVICE
Detroit, Mich., January 15, 1917.

DEAR SIR: We have just passed through a year of great prosperity. What will this year bring? The present outlook is for a year more prosperous than its predecessor, but this is an ominous outlook for a year full of strife and struggles between capital and labor.

In the last year labor organizations made more headway in organizing in the city of Detroit than had been done in any ten previous years; and a grand final effort will be made to swing many more workers into the ranks of labor unions to prepare for a general strike which is contemplated for May 1917.

Are you, a representative manufacturer of the city of Detroit, going to allow your shop to be organized? You owe it to your concern and the other manufacturers of this city to do your part in suppressing the proposed unionization of your employees. Possibly you do not fully realize, being in an open-shop town, just what union domination means. If not, ask some manufacturer of Chicago or San Francisco where for a number of years the manufacturers were dominated by the unions and their hirelings.

If you act now, you can do your part in helping to combat this proposed strike and reduce the efforts of the labor agitators to a minimum of results. Preparedness against labor agitators is an absolute business necessity at this time. Allow us to call upon you and tell you how we can assist you in keeping your plant free from agitators.

Thanking you for an interview, we remain,

Yours for service,

E. J. McCOLLISTER,
General Manager.

FOSTER SERVICE,
New York, July 30, 1920.

Mr. _____
_____ Co., New York City.

Dear Sir: Your letter of July 28 is received. With reference to your inquiry about my experience and what I am prepared to do in case of disturbance, etc.:

* U.S. Congress, Senate, Subcommittee of the Committee on Education and Labor, *Hearings, Violations of Free Speech and Assembly and Interference with Rights of Labor.* 74th Cong., 2d Sess., 1936, pp. 70, 71.

First. I will say that if we are employed before any union or organization is formed by the employees, there will be no strike and no disturbance. This does not say that there will be no unions formed, but it does say that we will control the activities of the union and direct its policies, provided we are allowed a free hand by our clients.

Second. If a union is already formed and no strike is on or expected to be declared within thirty to sixty days, although we are not in the same position as we would be in the above case, we could—and I believe with success—carry on an intrigue which would result in factions, disagreement, resignations of officers, and general decrease in the membership; and if a strike were called, we would be in a position to furnish information, etc., of contemplated assaults.

If a strike is already on, I am not so sure of being of much material assistance, because the bars are up against all newcomers and everyone looks upon you with an eye of suspicion. Of course, it is possible that we might be of some material assistance, but the percentage is too high against us to be encouraging to our clients. Of course, if we were just looking for your money and nothing else, we would not be so particular in setting forth our limits.

Every one of our investigators is of high caliber and is made to feel that he is part of the business and permanently in our employ as long as he is faithful in the performance of his duty. Their success means our success and that of our clients.

As to experience, I will say I have rubbed elbows with all classes of society, do not "carry a chip on my shoulder," and believe in the motto that "molasses instead of vinegar" in many cases brings results. This does not necessarily say that we would dodge danger or desert our post in time of danger. Far from it. An experience of seventeen years in my present field has taught me that you must give the other fellow credit for being as clever as yourself, if you want to be a success.

A conference with me will cost you nothing, if you are in the city, and you can then judge for yourself whether it is desirable to retain us.

Yours truly,

ROBERT J. FOSTER.

The Professional Strikebreaker (1936) *

Senator LA FOLLETTE. Where did you work in June and July of 1934?
Mr. McDADE. Milwaukee, Wisconsin.

* From the testimony of E. J. McDade, September 23, 1936. U.S. Congress, Senate, Subcommittee of the Committee on Education and Labor, *Hearings, Violations of Free Speech and Rights of Labor*, 74th Cong., 2d Sess., 1936, Part 1: Labor Espionage and Strikebreaking, pp. 125-128.

Senator LA FOLLETTE. What agency did you work for?

Mr. McDADE. Bergoff Service Bureau.

Senator LA FOLLETTE. Anyone else?

Mr. McDADE. Well, I was working at the time for the Wisconsin Light and Power Co.

Senator LA FOLLETTE. How many strikebreakers were on that job?

Mr. McDADE. About 700.

Senator LA FOLLETTE. Where were they brought from?

Mr. McDADE. Chicago and New York City.

Senator LA FOLLETTE. Who brought them in?

Mr. McDADE. The Bergoff Service Bureau.

Senator LA FOLLETTE. The Bergoff Service Bureau recruited the strikebreakers?

Mr. McDADE. Yes, sir.

Senator LA FOLLETTE. How were they transported in?

Mr. McDADE. Well, the first recruiting originated in Chicago, and they did not have enough men down there, they thought they would have trouble with the generating plant outside of Milwaukee—there were 300 down there then—and they ordered 400 more and we could not get the men in Chicago, and the president of the company advised them to place an order to New York City to bring them in by plane if necessary.

Senator LA FOLLETTE. The president of what company?

Mr. McDADE. Wisconsin Light & Power.

Senator LA FOLLETTE. How was the recruiting done for these men on this Milwaukee job? Where did you pick these fellows up?

Mr. McDADE. Sometimes they picked them up at men's hotels, poolrooms.

Senator LA FOLLETTE. What kind of hotels?

Mr. McDADE. Men's hotels, cheap hotels, poolrooms, sometimes employment agencies—that is, for the men that are actually going to go to work down there.

Senator LA FOLLETTE. Do men hang around places of that kind in the hope that they are going to be recruited for jobs like this?

Mr. McDADE. Some men do; yes.

Senator LA FOLLETTE. They make it a regular business?

Mr. McDADE. Yes.

Senator LA FOLLETTE. And they know where to hang out in order to be in touch with the various agencies that might be looking for strikebreakers?

Mr. McDADE. Yes, sir.

Senator LA FOLLETTE. Do you make any effort to find out what the character of these men is?

Mr. McDADE. No, sir.

Senator LA FOLLETTE. They often pick up fellows that have police records?

Mr. McDADE. Yes, sir.

Senator LA FOLLETTE. That is quite common, is it?

Mr. McDADE. Yes, sir.

Senator LA FOLLETTE. What were your duties on this Milwaukee job?

Mr. McDADE. I brought some men in, brought several bus loads of men in from Chicago.

Senator LA FOLLETTE. Just tell us how you went about it. When you heard they wanted a couple of bus loads of men tell the committee just how you went about it in Chicago to pick them up.

Mr. McDADE. They were turned over to me in the office down there. It was my job to bring them in by bus.

Senator LA FOLLETTE. The Bergoff office in Chicago told you they would turn the men over to you?

Mr. McDADE. Yes.

Senator LA FOLLETTE. Do you know, as a matter of your own knowledge—do you know how they went about getting these men? What did they do? Did they just go down Halstead Street, and streets like that, and pass the word around that they needed a bunch of strikebreakers for the job?

Mr. McDADE. Yes.

Senator LA FOLLETTE. When you got to Milwaukee, what job did you have?

Mr. McDADE. I brought the men to the power plant outside of Milwaukee.

Senator LA FOLLETTE. And turned them over to whom?

Mr. McDADE. Well, I stayed right there with them.

Senator LA FOLLETTE. You were a sort of a boss of that particular bus load, or two bus loads of men?

Mr. McDADE. Yes, sir.

Senator LA FOLLETTE. Were those men actually put to work?

Mr. McDADE. No, sir.

Senator LA FOLLETTE. What did they do with those three or four hundred men?

Mr. McDADE. They told them to stand near the fences and keep the people out in case there was a crush in.

Senator LA FOLLETTE. Were they armed?

Mr. McDADE. No, sir; not down there.

Senator LA FOLLETTE. Did you carry arms on this job?

Mr. McDADE. No, sir.

Senator La Follette. Were you deputized?

Mr. McDade. No, sir.

Senator La Follette. Were any of these men deputized?

Mr. McDade. No, sir.

Senator La Follette. Not during the entire strike?

Mr. McDade. No, sir.

Senator La Follette. Now, how did the company go about protecting the plant, if you know?

Mr. McDade. Against the pickets?

Senator La Follette. Yes; against the pickets.

Mr. McDade. Well, they furnished the men with pickax handles.

Senator La Follette. Pickax handles?

Mr. McDade. Yes.

Senator La Follette. They passed them out to about 700 men?

Mr. McDade. Well, there was not 700 in that particular spot; there were about 200.

Senator La Follette. I am talking about the job. On that particular job they had about 700 strikebreakers?

Mr. McDade. This is on the whole job.

Senator La Follette. Did they pass out pickax handles to all of them?

Mr. McDade. I do not know about outside. We were just at the power plant there.

Senator La Follette. You were just at the power plant?

Mr. McDade. Yes.

Senator La Follette. Did you hear about their being armed elsewhere?

Mr. McDade. No, sir.

Senator La Follette. And what other protection did the company install there?

Mr. McDade. Steam hoses connected up with boilers.

Senator La Follette. So they could turn live steam on the pickets?

Mr. McDade. Yes, sir.

Senator La Follette. Any other protection?

Mr. McDade. That is about all.

Senator La Follette. Are you sure of that?

Mr. McDade. Yes, sir.

Senator La Follette. Were there any wires concealed anywhere?

Mr. McDade. I did not see the wires, but they say there was. There was somebody electrocuted down there one night.

Senator La Follette. Were those wires strung for that protection purpose?

Mr. McDade. I believe they were.

Senator LA FOLLETTE. Were they concealed?

Mr. McDADE. They must have been.

Senator LA FOLLETTE. They were? Was anybody hurt?

Mr. McDADE. Yes, sir; there were two men hurt and one young man was killed.

Senator LA FOLLETTE. Two men hurt and one young man killed?

Mr. McDADE. Yes.

Senator LA FOLLETTE. Was he electrocuted by this concealed wire?

Mr. McDADE. Yes, sir.

Senator LA FOLLETTE. Do you know who placed that wire?

Mr. McDADE. No, sir; I do not.

Senator LA FOLLETTE. Do you know whether it was done by the company or the agency?

Mr. McDADE. I did not even know that it was done until after it happened.

Senator LA FOLLETTE. But if it was done by either one it must have been done with the consent of the company, or otherwise they could not have gotten the wire hooked up to the juice, could they?

Mr. McDADE. I do not know anything about that.

Senator LA FOLLETTE. Did you have any conversations with the president of the company?

Mr. McDADE. There was a conversation one morning at four o'clock.

Senator LA FOLLETTE. What was his name?

Mr. McDADE. Way.

Senator LA FOLLETTE. Are his initials S. B.?

Mr. McDADE. Yes, sir.

Senator LA FOLLETTE. How did he feel about the work that these strikebreakers were doing with their pickax handles and concealed wires?

Mr. McDADE. Well, after the man was electrocuted, he worried about a general march in from Milwaukee of sympathizers to wreck the plant.

Senator LA FOLLETTE. Not employees, but just general sympathizers?

Mr. McDADE. Yes, sir.

Senator LA FOLLETTE. Well, was he satisfied with the work you were doing, aside from the fact that there had been this aroused public opinion against the company?

Mr. McDADE. No, sir; he wanted more men.

Senator LA FOLLETTE. He wanted more men?

Mr. McDADE. Yes.

Senator LA FOLLETTE. What comments did he make?

Mr. McDADE. Well, he was under the impression there would be a riot the night following the murder. . . .

Labor Espionage, Inc. (1936) *

Senator LA FOLLETTE. What sort of a business did these corporations do?

Mr. LAWSON. The National Corporation Service did special investigations and employed men in various manufacturing plants as stool pigeons. The Allied Corporation Service was a strikebreaking organization.

Senator LA FOLLETTE. Will you explain the difference between those two types of business?

Mr. LAWSON. Well, under the National Corporation we hired men or hooked men in plants to furnish information in reference to union activities and to ascertain the feeling of the men in the plants as to the management, for the purpose of taking up the question of increases in wages. The Allied Corporation Service was an out-and-out strikebreaking organization and handled no other work but strikes.

Senator LA FOLLETTE. Which was the larger portion of the business of the National Corporation Service, this investigative work that you spoke of or this labor espionage?

Mr. LAWSON. Labor espionage. There was very little special investigation work.

Senator LA FOLLETTE. When was the National Corporation Service formed, if you remember?

Mr. LAWSON. In March 1931.

Senator LA FOLLETTE. And the Allied Corporation Service?

Mr. LAWSON. In March 1934.

Senator LA FOLLETTE. What were your duties as secretary? Were you also office manager?

Mr. LAWSON. I was office manager, kept the books, prepared all State, county, and Federal tax returns, and for quite some time assigned operatives' numbers and kept in touch with the operatives.

Senator LA FOLLETTE. Did you bill the clients?

Mr. LAWSON. Billed the clients, prepared the payrolls.

Senator LA FOLLETTE. Did you ever have anything to do with the assigning of operators to jobs?

Mr. LAWSON. In some cases, yes.

* From the testimony of A. E. Lawson, ex-secretary and accountant for the National Corporation Service, Inc. and the Allied Corporation Service, Inc., September 23, 1936. U.S. Congress, Senate, Subcommittee of the Committee on Education and Labor, *Hearings, Violations of Free Speech and Rights of Labor,* 74th Cong., 2d Sess., 1936, Part 1: Labor Espionage and Strikebreaking, pp. 177-183, 189, 190, 192, 195, 196.

Senator LA FOLLETTE. And did you keep a list or a record of all the operatives?

Mr. LAWSON. Yes, sir. . . .

Senator LA FOLLETTE. Well, I take it that your duties made you thoroughly familiar with the operatives for each client and the name of each of the operatives and his duties?

Mr. LAWSON. I did.

Senator LA FOLLETTE. Were you acquainted with the way in which the business was built up by Mr. MacGuffin?

Mr. LAWSON. Yes; I was. When I went with Mr. MacGuffin there was very little business, and I was there while the business was built up to the amount that it was in 1934.

Senator LA FOLLETTE. Tell us how they built the business up.

Mr. LAWSON. We had one salesman or solicitor for business during 1931, 1932, and 1933. Then we put on a superintendent of sales and three or four other salesmen, sent them broadcast throughout the State of Ohio and western Pennsylvania to see if they could not get more business.

Senator LA FOLLETTE. Did you find in your experience with this company that the condition of labor difficulties helped to swell business any?

Mr. LAWSON. Certainly.

Senator LA FOLLETTE. Now, when there were not any labor troubles, can you tell us how you got business then?

Mr. LAWSON. Well, we sold the business on a proposition of business insurance, "Protect yourself and find out what is going on in your plant before trouble actually does occur."

Senator LA FOLLETTE. Did you ever have occasions where the client would be assured in a situation of that kind that something could be done in the way of helping to build up company unions?

Mr. LAWSON. Yes; I know of such cases.

Senator LA FOLLETTE. Well, if you know of any of those I would like to have you explain to us in more detail just what was done in that regard.

Mr. LAWSON. We put men in the Newton Steel Co. at Newton Falls just after the plant was reopened for business and formed a company union there. We also formed a company union in the Taylor Winfield Co. at Warren, Ohio, to offset any possibility of joining the outside union.

Senator LA FOLLETTE. How did they go about setting up these company unions, if you know?

Mr. LAWSON. Well, they would put one man in as a leader, furnish him information as to bylaws and regulations of the company union.

Senator LA FOLLETTE. Who usually prepared the bylaws, and so forth?

Mr. LAWSON. Well, we had probably fifteen or twenty different setups from other manufacturing plants.

Senator LA FOLLETTE. You would sell the client the one he liked best?

Mr. LAWSON. We would sell him the one that we thought would fit the plant best.

Senator LA FOLLETTE. You usually got his approval of it before you started up?

Mr. LAWSON. Oh, certainly.

Senator LA FOLLETTE. Did you have any ways and means of keeping track of where difficulties were likely to break out in regard to the labor situation?

Mr. LAWSON. Oh, yes.

Senator LA FOLLETTE. How did you do that?

Mr. LAWSON. Well, we had two or three men that wrote us reports on general conditions around throughout the plants that they were working in and from various unions that they were connected with. . . .

Senator LA FOLLETTE. And what were the occupations or positions of these men that you mentioned as being typical of your sources of information?

Mr. LAWSON. One of them was financial secretary of the Machinists' Union and another was secretary of the Moulders' Union, and Cross was an organizer of the M.E.S.A.

Senator LA FOLLETTE. What is the M.E.S.A.?

Mr. LAWSON. Mechanics' Educational Society of America, with headquarters in Detroit.

Senator LA FOLLETTE. Were they in the main offices?

Mr. LAWSON. No; they were in the local offices.

Senator LA FOLLETTE. Now, how do you follow the sales development?

Mr. LAWSON. From the orders that were turned in by the salesmen and the assignment of new operatives.

Senator LA FOLLETTE. What did you find to be the principal problem, as far as keeping the business after you got it sold?

Mr. LAWSON. To furnish the information the client was looking for and keep him satisfied.

Senator LA FOLLETTE. Well, how did you do that? How did you keep him satisfied?

Mr. LAWSON. Well, the first reports we would get from an operative did not amount to much, but they were educated as to how to write up a report, and these reports then were sent in to the clients, and if they had any special thing that they wanted us to locate in the plant we would turn it over to the operative and have him work on that.

Senator LA FOLLETTE. How did you keep track of the strike situation?

Mr. LAWSON. Well, that would come through information we had received from some of our operatives. They might know where a strike was brewing from the trouble that would be stirred up in their union, or we had telephone calls on strike work.

Senator LA FOLLETTE. When you heard that a strike was brewing somewhere, what did you do then?

Mr. LAWSON. Sent a salesman out to interview the prospective client to see if we could not sell him the service.

Senator LA FOLLETTE. Were you sometimes solicited by clients? I mean did they first take the initiative in getting in touch with you?

Mr. LAWSON. We have had such things happen.

Senator LA FOLLETTE. Are you familiar with the term "hooking"?

Mr. LAWSON. Yes.

Senator LA FOLLETTE. Is that a common term in the business?

Mr. LAWSON. A common term as far as I know about it.

Senator LA FOLLETTE. Did you have anything to do with hooking?

Mr. LAWSON. No; I did not. . . .

Senator LA FOLLETTE. Do you know about the way in which they trained operatives in this business?

Mr. LAWSON. Oh, not very much; only they would get a man hooked in a plant, they would educate him as to the information they wanted and how the report should be written.

Senator LA FOLLETTE. Is it hard for a man to get unhooked or is it easy?

Mr. LAWSON. Well, I would say it would be hard to get unhooked.

Senator LA FOLLETTE. Why?

Mr. LAWSON. Because you do not know what the reaction would be after you had been hooked as an "op."

Senator LA FOLLETTE. As an operative you mean?

Mr. LAWSON. As an operative; yes.

Senator LA FOLLETTE. You mean once a man is hooked and you have got his receipt for money received he is in a little embarrassing position?

Mr. LAWSON. He is always very anxious to continue the business.

Senator LA FOLLETTE. In general, was it the practice to try to hook men in the plants of a client, or did you put your own outside operatives in usually?

Mr. LAWSON. Well, in many cases where you could not put your own outside operatives in; yes.

Senator La Follette. You mean he would be suspected?

Mr. Lawson. He would be suspected, and then you had to hook an operative in a plant.

Senator La Follette. How many operatives did you keep records on during the time you were with this company, if you remember, approximately?

Mr. Lawson. Somewhere close to 300 employees.

Senator La Follette. Could you tell us what percentage of those men were hooked men?

Mr. Lawson. About seventy percent.

Senator La Follette. I am sure the committee would be interested in knowing how you recruit for a strikebreaking job.

Mr. Lawson. How we what?

Senator La Follette. How do they recruit for a strikebreaking job?

Mr. Lawson. We had a man by the name of John McCabe with the Allied Corporation Service who was experienced on that kind of work and all he had to do was put the word out in Cleveland, New York, or Chicago and we could get all the strikebreakers we needed.

Senator La Follette. Do you understand the term "fink"?

Mr. Lawson. Yes, sir.

Senator La Follette. Is that a common word in the business?

Mr. Lawson. It is.

Senator La Follette. What is a fink?

Mr. Lawson. A strikebreaker.

Senator La Follette. Do they ever use employment agencies; do you know?

Mr. Lawson. Sometimes; yes.

Senator La Follette. And after they get into the business of strikebreaking do they keep records or do they not keep records of finks, or strikebreakers, the company itself?

Mr. Lawson. Oh, yes; we have always had a record of our finks.

Senator La Follette. Is it quite customary where you get a strikebreaking job to ship these men in interstate commerce from one state into another?

Mr. Lawson. Yes, sir.

Senator La Follette. What are the principal sources, so far as you know, of recruiting finks, or strikebreakers.

Mr. Lawson. The two main points are Chicago and New York.

Senator La Follette. And other subsidiary points would be what?

Mr. Lawson. Other subsidiary points would be Cleveland, and we did pick up a few men in Columbus, and Newcastle, Pennsylvania.

Senator La Follette. Now, what types of men do they get for the strikebreaking work? Do they make any careful survey of their qualifications and their character?

Mr. LAWSON. They take anybody that comes along. . . .

Senator LA FOLLETTE. Were you familiar with the Newton Steel Co. operations at Newton Falls and Monroe, Michigan?

Mr. LAWSON. Yes, sir.

Senator LA FOLLETTE. Who was the operative there?

Mr. LAWSON. We had eleven of them at Newton Falls.

Senator LA FOLLETTE. Were they connected with the union?

Mr. LAWSON. They went in before the union was formed. We had seven men in there to form a company union, and four to do general reporting and giving us the backfire on the progress of the company union.

Senator LA FOLLETTE. Did one of your operatives become an officer of the company union after it was formed?

Mr. LAWSON. Yes, sir.

Senator LA FOLLETTE. What office did he hold?

Mr. LAWSON. I believe he was secretary.

Senator LA FOLLETTE. Was it ever a practice after you got a man into a union, company or otherwise, to get the union to issue cards to other operatives?

Mr. LAWSON. That has been done; yes. . . .

Senator LA FOLLETTE. Are you familiar with the Johnson Bronze Co. job?

Mr. LAWSON. Yes, sir.

Senator LA FOLLETTE. What kind of a job is that?

Mr. LAWSON. That was a strike job and inside operatives and street operatives.

Senator LA FOLLETTE. I have heard that term before. What is a "street operative"?

Mr. LAWSON. Operatives that work out on the outside of the plant to get general information.

Senator LA FOLLETTE. Does that fall under the head of so-called missionary work?

Mr. LAWSON. Well, some people might call it that.

Senator LA FOLLETTE. What do they usually do? What do these street operatives do on a job like this usually?

Mr. LAWSON. Contact people around the town to see how they feel about the conditions—contact employees' wives or mothers at their homes.

Senator LA FOLLETTE. Break down morale?

Mr. LAWSON. And break down morale. . . .

Senator LA FOLLETTE. What do you remember about the Goodrich Tire & Rubber Co., Account No. 2038? . . .

Mr LAWSON. That was general labor espionage.

Senator LA FOLLETTE. How about the Firestone Tire & Rubber Co., Account No. 2081?

Mr. LAWSON. Special reports on union meetings.

Senator LA FOLLETTE. Do you know of any instances in which it was the practice for your operatives to create a disturbance?

Mr. LAWSON. I know of one instance there; yes.

Senator LA FOLLETTE. Tell us about it.

Mr. LAWSON. There was four or five men sent to Akron to try to raise a disturbance in a union meeting which was to be held in a public school.

Senator LA FOLLETTE. What was the purpose of that?

Mr. LAWSON. It was to break up that union. The union was figuring on requesting an advance in wages, and holding these meetings in the public school, if it would bring it to the attention of the people, if there was a disturbance raised there, that the schools were no place to hold such meetings. And as there was not any hall in Akron large enough to accommodate the crowds they had at the meetings it would kind of slow down their union meetings.

Senator LA FOLLETTE. Do you know whether it was accomplished?

Mr. LAWSON. It was; yes. And two of our men were arrested. . . .

Senator THOMAS. In some of the other witnesses that have been before us there seemed to be almost a pride of particular occupation developed. For instance, this morning one of the witnesses did not like the committee to use the word "scab" in speaking of a strikebreaker. Is there an esprit de corps and a morale among these men?

Mr. LAWSON. Not that I know of. I don't know what the difference would be between a scab and a strikebreaker.

Senator THOMAS. This morning a witness said a strikebreaker never took another man's job, he just went in and acted like a workman instead of being a workman.

Mr. LAWSON. Don't ninety-five percent of them act like a workman instead of being a workman?

Senator THOMAS. There could be such a thing as an honest scab, couldn't there?

Mr. LAWSON. I believe so.

Senator THOMAS. You do not find them often?

Mr. LAWSON. Not very often.

Senator THOMAS. Do you find honest strikebreakers?

Mr. LAWSON. Few and far between.

Senator THOMAS. These men have made up their minds to make this their life's work?

Mr. LAWSON. They work at it for years, but there is always something wrong with most of them, or they wouldn't be in that business. . . .

Senator LA FOLLETTE. Mr. Lawson, are you glad to be out of this business?

Mr. LAWSON. I certainly am.

Senator LA FOLLETTE. That is all.

A Hooker (1936) *

Senator LA FOLLETTE. Have you ever done any hooking or roping?

Mr. KUHL. Yes, sir.

Senator LA FOLLETTE. How do you do that?

Mr. KUHL. Well, first you look your prospect over, and if he is married that is preferable. If he is financially hard up, that is number two. If his wife wants more money or he hasn't got a car, that all counts. And you go offer him this extra money, naturally you don't tell him what you want him for. You have got some story that you are representing some bankers or some bondholders or an insurance company and they want to know what goes on in there.

You probably tell him, "I want to know more of what these foremen and superintendents do than your fellow workmen."

Well, if he goes along and plays ball, and I think maybe seventy percent, or next to it, from the start know, but in no time at all, say, ninety per cent, say, in two or three months, know what they are really doing, because you have got to go back to this fellow and school him and train him to bring in facts that this particular client wants to know. And today it is all as regards unions and the activities of unions.

Senator LA FOLLETTE. That is most of the work now?

Mr. KUHL. That is most of the work.

Senator LA FOLLETTE. After a fellow gets hooked, suppose he wants to get unhooked; is that difficult for him?

Mr. KUHL. Well, if he is a good man and you don't want to lose him, because they are hard to hook, you will try to keep him with you. You have his receipts, and probably he will sign a receipt with a number, and he says, "Aw, hell, that don't mean anything. That is only a number."

* From the testimony of C. M. Kuhl of Youngstown, Ohio, a former employee of the national Corporation Service, the Allied Corporation Service, the Central Industrial Service, and the Railway Audit & Inspection Co., September 23, 1936. U.S. Congress, Senate, Subcommittee of the Committee on Education and Labor, *Hearings, Violations of Free Speech and Rights of Labor,* 74th Cong., 2d Sess., 1936, Part 1: Labor Espionage and Strikebreaking, p. 201.

But still you have his handwriting where he wrote in his original reports. And in some cases, if the fellow really wants to become unhooked he can become unhooked.

Senator THOMAS. Does he know that?

Mr. KUHL. No; he don't know it. What I mean is if he comes right out and says, "I am done with this," why, he can be done with it.

Senator LA FOLLETTE. Did you ever hook any men who objected after they found out what you really wanted of them?

Mr. KUHL. No; I don't believe I did. I have hooked men after——

Senator LA FOLLETTE (interposing). Is the turnover pretty large among the hooked men?

Mr. KUHL. Yes; there is a large number of hooked men, but after they become hooked there is a large percentage that stay that way. You know, they will go from one job to another or from one city to another.

THE ARSENAL OF RESISTANCE

Lake Erie Chemical Co. (1936) *

Senator LA FOLLETTE. What is the business of the Lake Erie Chemical Co., briefly?

Mr. AILES. They manufacture tear gas equipment, heavier ordnance that enters into export business, police equipment, and sell engineering service. . . .

Senator LA FOLLETTE. What type of gas weapons does your company manufacture and sell?

Mr. AILES. Shoulder gas guns on down to small individual weapons for the protection of an individual against attack, and tear gas grenades of all sorts. . . .

Senator LA FOLLETTE. Will you look at exhibit 204, please, Mr. Ailes? It is a copy of an internal letter of the Lake Erie Chemical Co., Cleveland, Ohio, July 1, 1936, from W. P. Northcott to A. S. Ailes; subject, steel industries. Is this a copy of a letter that you received from Mr. Northcott?

Mr. AILES. It is.

Senator LA FOLLETTE (reading):

* From the testimony of A. S. Ailes, Vice-President and Sales Manager of the Lake Erie Chemical Co., Cleveland, Ohio, September 24, 1936. U.S. Congress, Senate, Subcommittee of the Committee on Education and Labor, *Hearings, Violations of Free Speech and Rights of Labor,* 74th Cong., 2d Sess., 1936, Part 2: Labor Espionage and Strikebreaking, pp. 388, 397-400, 411-414.

DEAR MR. AILES: The proposed drive for the unionization of this trade will certainly stir up a lot of trouble sooner or later.

I am keeping in close touch with the United States Steel Corporation headquarters in Chicago, which, as you are aware, includes the many subsidiary companies. . . .

If you have any line on any strikes or threats of strikes in my territory or vicinity, I hope you will post me as soon as you learn of it.

Yours very truly,

W. P. N.

Is it your custom to keep the agents of the company posted on developments of that nature?

Mr. AILES: It is. . . .

Senator LA FOLLETTE. Will you please look at exhibit 205, Mr. Ailes? . . .

(Western Union telegram, day letter)

CLEVELAND, OHIO, *May 10, 1935.*

L. C. RAWLINS,
4805 Kingsessing Avenue, Philadelphia, Pa.:

Watch strike marine workers and shipbuilders, Camden, and advise if we should move some material to Philadelphia. Specialize on Jumper Repeaters. Limited amount long range guns on hand; plenty of shells, however. Advise.

AILES,
LAKE ERIE CHEMICAL COMPANY

Chg. 5806 Hough Ave.
9:10
asa:eb

Senator LA FOLLETTE. Will you look at exhibit 208, please, Mr. Ailes? . . .

HERRICK FOOTE,
NEW HAVEN, CONN., *June 15, 1935.*

A. S. AILES,
Lake Erie Chemical Company, Cleveland, Ohio

DEAR MR. AILES: I beg to advise you that a meeting of the national officials of the United Textile Workers Union of America held at Providence, R.I., yesterday demanded a 20% increase in wages for the workers in the cotton and woolen mills and if this 20% increase was not given within the next ten days, a general strike throughout the country would be called. This looks like some business and if this strike matures, it will be a bad one. Hope you have something definite as to the new long range gun, as we will be in a bad way, if this strike gets under way and we have no long range guns.

Had you developed the True Flite Gun and shell at that time?

Mr. AILES. What is the date of that?

Senator LA FOLLETTE. June 1935.

Mr. AILES. I don't think so.

Senator LA FOLLETTE (reading):

What demonstrations I have had of the Jumper-Repeater Candles, show the police officials are impressed and think that this particular munition is just the cats meows.

Does it make any noise when it goes off?

Mr. AILES. Yes; it does.

Senator LA FOLLETTE. Does it sound like a cat meowing?

Mr. AILES. No.

Senator LA FOLLETTE (reading):

I hope that this strike develops and matures and that it will be a damn bad one, we need the money.
Awaiting your reply, I am,
    Very truly yours,

HERRICK FOOTE.

And then he adds:

Everyone wants to be up on their toes watching this situation and work fast.

Do you make sales to detective agencies?

Mr. AILES. Sometimes.

Senator LA FOLLETTE. Do they ever act as your agents in the sale of materials?

Mr. AILES. We have no established relationship with any detective agency to act in a sales capacity.

Senator LA FOLLETTE. Do you give detective agencies a more favorable discount than other customers?

Mr. AILES. We might.

Senator LA FOLLETTE. What is the usual quantity discount?

Mr. AILES. Oh, five percent in lots of two dozen on grenades, ten per cent on lots of one hundred, twenty in lots of one thousand. That is a quantity discount. . . .

Senator THOMAS. Mr. Chairman, before Mr. Ailes leaves the stand I would like to ask him one or two questions.

First of all, Mr. Ailes, you are primarily a salesman, aren't you?

Mr. AILES. I do a little direct selling myself. I am the sales manager.

Senator THOMAS. Are you a chemical engineer?

Mr. AILES. I am not.

Senator THOMAS. Have you studied medicine?

Mr. AILES. I have not.

Senator THOMAS. Have you ever seen anyone gassed?

Mr. AILES. I have.

Senator THOMAS. Where?

Mr. AILES. Well, I have been gassed myself a thousand times. We do it continually experimentally on our own people and ourselves. I have seen it in riots.

Senator THOMAS. It is just a harmless proposition, then, is it?

Mr. AILES. It depends entirely on the circumstances. The gas itself in ordinary concentrations is harmless.

That does not mean that you can't be injured by the discharges of the gas. We make no claim that it is a harmless proposition. . . .

Senator THOMAS. Therefore, you cannot just use gas promiscuously, can you?

Mr. AILES. I should say you could not.

Senator THOMAS. You have already mentioned the fact that there is a certain technique that goes with the use of gas. What do you think of the moral obligations of an organization which decides to use gas and does not train men in its use?

Mr. AILES. I think they have simply been neglectful. If they wait until somebody tears down their factory before they put gas in the hands of the men, they can expect to get in trouble.

Senator THOMAS. We have had in the last two or three days some testimony from men who call themselves "nobles," "finks," "guards," and ordinary strikebreakers. Does a manufacturer or does a detective agency have no responsibility at all in giving over to these men the handling of gas projectiles?

Mr. AILES. I presume they have a responsibility. But there are many factories that have no plant personnel to protect themselves in case there is an attack upon the factory; and I know of nothing else they can do except go to an outside organization and take what they can get. . . .

Senator THOMAS. Haven't you testified here, or have you not considered the fact, that the rougher the times or the more trouble, the better the sale?

Mr. AILES. That is not in my letters. I cannot be responsible for these ramblings of irresponsible salesmen in letters to me.

Senator THOMAS. Well, you have never been happy to discover that there are strikes?

Mr. AILES. I cannot say that I have.

Senator THOMAS. Can you say that you have not?

Mr. AILES. Yes; I can say that I have not.

Senator THOMAS. Just as a matter of course?

Mr. AILES. I am sorry that there are strikes; that there have to be strikes. I am sorry there are Communists in the country. If we did not have a lot of those birds I would not be in this business. The manufacturers have a side to this question as well as the strikers. When they tear down factories and bring 500 rifles on the property of the manufacturers and shoot people through the stomach and refuse to let doctors treat them, I think it is time to use gas, bullets, or something else.

Senator THOMAS. I think there are two sides to the striking business, and we want to bring out both sides.

Mr. AILES. I hope you do bring out both sides.

V. Organizing the Unorganized: The 1930's

CIO

Emboldened by favorable government legislation, an increasingly sympathetic public, and the militancy of the newly formed C.I.O., labor organizers invaded the strongholds of antiunionism in the 1930's. That the weapons of resistance, described in the previous section, could be effectively employed to combat unionism was made abundantly evident in many industrial areas. But this time labor refused to give up, accepting momentary defeats only to come back and try again. The result was what *Fortune* magazine described as "Industrial War," culminating in the attempted unionization of the steel industry, long considered an impregnable fortress. Open warfare was not new to labor, but at no time was it more pronounced or widespread than in the 1930's. And at no previous time had the issues been so clearcut—recognition and collective bargaining.

Talking Union (1941) *

by the Almanac Singers
(Talking blues, steady beat)

If you want higher wages, let me tell you what to do,
You've got to talk to the workers in the shop with you.
You've got to build you a union, got to make it strong,
But if you all stick together, boys, 'twon't be long—
You'll get shorter hours . . . better working conditions . . .
Vacations with pay . . . take your kids to the seashore.

It ain't quite this simple, so I'd better explain
Just why you've got to ride on the union train,
'Cause if you wait for the boss to raise your pay

We'll all be a-waiting till the judgment day—
We'll all be buried . . . gone to heaven . . .
St. Peter'll be the foreman then.

Now you know you're underpaid but the boss says you ain't,
He speeds up the work till you're about to faint.
You may be down and out, but you ain't beaten—
You can pass out a leaflet and call a meetin'—
Talk it over . . . speak your mind . . .
Decide to do something about it.

Suppose they're working you so hard it's just outrageous,
And they're paying you all starvation wages.
You go to the boss and the boss will yell
"Before I raise your pay I'll see you all in Hell."

'Course, the boss may persuade some poor damn fool
To go to your meeting and act like a stool,
But you can always tell a stool, boys, that's a fact,
He's got a yellow streak a-running down his back.
He doesn't have to stool . . . he'll always get along . . .
On what he steals out of blind men's cups.

You've got a union now and you're sitting pretty;
Put some of the boys on the bargaining committee.
The boss won't listen when one guy squawks
But he's got to listen when the union talks.
He'd better . . . be mighty lonely . . .
If everybody decided to walk out on him.

He's puffing a big seegar, feeling mighty slick
'Cause he thinks he's got your union licked.
Well, he looks out the window, and what does he see
But a thousand pickets, and they all agree
He's a bastard . . . unfair . . . slave-driver . . .
Bet he beats his wife.

Now, boys, you've come to the hardest time
The boss will try to bust your picket line.
He'll call out the po-lice and the National Guard;
They'll tell you it's a crime to have a union card;

They'll raid your meetings, they'll hit you on the head—
They'll call every one of you a Goddamn Red—
Unpatriotic . . . agitators . . .
Send 'em back where they came from.

But out in De-troit, here's what they found,
And out in Pittsburgh, here's what they found,
And out in Akron, here's what they found,
And up in Toronto, here's what they found;
That if you don't let Red-baiting break you up,
And if you don't let vigilantes break you up,
And if you don't let race hatred break you up,
And if you don't let stool-pigeons break you up,
You'll win . . . what I mean . . .
Take it easy . . . but take it!

THE LEGAL BASIS

Norris-La Guardia Act (1932) *

Sec. 2. In the interpretation of this Act and in determining the jurisdiction and authority of the courts of the United States, as such jurisdiction and authority are herein defined and limited, the public policy of the United States is hereby declared as follows:

Whereas under prevailing economic conditions, developed with the aid of governmental authority for owners of property to organize in the corporate and other forms of ownership association, the individual unorganized worker is commonly helpless to exercise actual liberty of contract and to protect his freedom of labor, and thereby to obtain acceptable terms and conditions of employment, wherefore, though he should be free to decline to associate with his fellows, it is necessary that he have full freedom of association, self-organization, and designation of representatives of his own choosing, to negotiate the terms and conditions of his employment, and that he shall be free from the interference, restraint, or coercion of employers of labor, or their agents, in the designation of such representatives or in self-organization or in other concerted activities for the purpose of collective bargaining or other mutual aid or protection; therefore, the following definitions of, and limitations upon, the jurisdiction and authority of the courts of the United States are

* From the Norris-La Guardia Act of 1932. 47 Stat. 70.

hereby enacted. [The act outlaws the "yellow-dog" contract and places restrictions on injunctions in labor disputes.]

National Industrial Recovery Act (1933) *

Sec. 7. (a) Every code of fair competition, agreement, and license approved, prescribed, or issued under this title shall contain the following conditions: (1) That employees shall have the right to organize and bargain collectively through representatives of their own choosing, and shall be free from the interference, restraint, or coercion of employers of labor, or their agents, in the designation of such representatives or in self-organization or in other concerted activities for the purpose of collective bargaining or other mutual aid or protection; (2) that no employee and no one seeking employment shall be required as a condition of employment to join any company union or to refrain from joining, organizing, or assisting a labor organization of his own choosing. . . .

National Labor Relations (Wagner) Act (1935) †

Sec. 1. . . . The inequality of bargaining power between employees who do not possess full freedom of association or actual liberty of contract, and employers who are organized in the corporate or other forms of ownership association substantially burdens and affects the flow of commerce, and tends to aggravate recurrent business depressions, by depressing wage rates and the purchasing power of wage earners in industry and by preventing the stabilization of competitive wage rates and working conditions within and between industries.

Experience has proved that protection by law of the right of employees to organize and bargain collectively safeguards commerce from injury, impairment, or interruption, and promotes the flow of commerce by removing certain recognized sources of industrial strife and unrest, by encouraging practices fundamental to the friendly adjustment of industrial disputes arising out of differences as to wages, hours, or other working conditions, and by restoring equality of bargaining power between employers and employees.

It is hereby declared to be the policy of the United States to eliminate

* From the National Industrial Recovery Act of 1933 (N.R.A.). 48 Stat. 198-199.

† From the National Labor Relations (Wagner) Act of 1935. 49 Stat. 449-450. An Act to diminish the causes of labor disputes burdening or obstructing interstate and foreign commerce, to create a National Labor Relations Board, and for other purposes.

the causes of certain substantial obstructions to the free flow of commerce and to mitigate and eliminate these obstructions when they have occurred by encouraging the practice and procedure of collective bargaining and by protecting the exercise by workers of full freedom of association, self-organization, and designation of representatives of their own choosing, for the purpose of negotiating the terms and conditions of their employment or other mutual aid or protection.

INDUSTRIAL WAR: *FORTUNE* MAGAZINE (1937) *

To progressive sociologists it is axiomatic that the United States, most advanced of the industrial nations, has had the least developed philosophy of labor. These people contend that until the present Administration took office, labor legislation in the United States, despite innumerable laws and commissions, has resulted in little essential change in organized labor's standing. They especially emphasize such significant facts as that before the current United States union drive, no more than eighteen per cent of United States nonagricultural labor was organized into trade unions, compared with over thirty-five per cent in Britain and more than seventy per cent in Sweden. And on the basis of these figures and various supplementary observations that we need not develop here, they hold that United States labor has lagged behind United States industry in the matter of self-fulfillment.

The United States businessman does not admit that his labor philosophy is backward. It is of course impossible to speak for *all* businessmen, and in attempting to speak for even a few one runs into insuperable difficulties in social terminology. . . . Here we can only say that in general, as the businessman sees it, this is a free country, with jobs open to all who can get them and the rights of private property inherent in every economic and political fiber. He has on the whole no "objection" to the organization of labor provided that this will not impede his free action as an owner (or representative of owners) of private property; provided he can hire and fire as he sees fit; provided his individual employees can work when they want to; provided, that is to say, that traditional labor relations are not materially changed. If an "advanced" labor philosophy presumes the existence of national labor unions that curtail this familiar freedom of action, then the average American businessman does not

* From "The Industrial War," *Fortune*, XVI (November, 1937), 105-110, 156, 158, 160, 166. Copyright 1937 by Time Inc. Reprinted by special permission.

want an advanced philosophy. Confronted with the possibility, or the threat, he takes his position upon the sturdy democratic tradition bequeathed to him by his forefathers, thus placing all those who are opposed to him in the awkward predicament of seeming to oppose that tradition. So that they become what Al Smith calls Communists.

Now whether you believe that this philosophy is backward, or whether you believe that it is the best that any democracy has so far devised, depends roughly upon which side of the private-property line your lot is cast. And as between those two irreconcilable extremes it is not the province of this article to choose. We are not here concerned with theory but with fact; the fact, namely, that for the past four and a half years the United States has been in the throes of a major labor upheaval, which can fairly be described as one of the greatest mass movements in our history. If one bars the irrepressible conflict of the Sixties, the only historical phenomenon comparable to the labor movement is the great trek westward, beginning in the Mississippi Valley and ending on the Pacific Coast. And if that classic American migration looms up to our generation as something far more permanent and vast it is well to remind ourselves that the labor movement likewise has a history. There has been labor unrest ever since there was a factory system, but the movement referred to here can properly be traced back to 1886-87, a period of open warfare characterized for the first time by a series of important strikes on the issue of the right to organize and bargain collectively through nationwide unions. The claim to that right, now widely conceded in Britain and the European democracies but still resisted in the United States, is the keystone of the American labor movement—is indeed what dignifies it as a movement rather than an intermittent and aimless war. Not that employers by and large are opposed to collective bargaining in principle. If they are involved in conflict, even as deeply involved as Mr. [Tom M.] Girdler [Chairman of Republic Steel Corporation], it is with national unions as instruments for achieving it. The various local unions and independent unions that many employers prefer are in themselves—since the passage of the Wagner Act—an important aspect of the industrial war; but we are here concerned with labor's longer attempt to achieve collective bargaining through nationwide unions such as are organized into the A.F. of L. and the C.I.O.

The history of that struggle can be had from any textbook and need not detain us here. At present we are considering its most modern phase—a phase that, corresponding roughly with the Roosevelt Administration, is in itself a compound affair illustrating an exceedingly rapid change. In the early days of the NRA there was no C.I.O., there was no Wagner Act, there was no La Follette Committee, and no Mohawk Valley

Formula; Big Steel had not yet "sold out" to labor; a sitdown strike had never been heard of in lay circles; and the American automobile was still for the most part innocent of unionized hands. Those things and those events were part of an evolution that was in its turn a part of the long labor movement above referred to. Not to understand this is to miss the point of every major event, every tactical decision, every judgment or error in judgment in the current labor world.

As a medical diagnosis can be reached only by a study of the symptoms, so it is necessary in an analysis of industrial warfare to reach into the heart of the problem by way of the strikes. For the strike is the external manifestation of labor's unrest, the thing that happens when an irresistible force meets an immovable body. . . .

From May, 1933, to July, 1937, a period of a little more than four years, there were some 10,000 strikes drawing out no less than 5,600,000 workers. This was aside from all the thousands of quickies, sitdowns, and other protests that tied up industry during that period—a "strike," as defined by the Department of Labor and used in this article, being an affair involving at least six workers for at least one day. . . . And perhaps most significant of all, there has been a marked trend in the causes of labor disputes, with the emphasis increasingly on the issue of union recognition. A labor movement fighting merely for better wages might or might not be a "movement" in the profound sense: it might be a kind of guerrilla warfare, indicating unrest but without historical direction. On the other hand, when men strike for union recognition, they are striking for collective bargaining, which we have already described as the keystone of the American labor movement. This collective bargaining theme has not always been to the fore by any means. Of the great 1919 strikes, only about twenty-four per cent were fought chiefly on this issue, while fifty-five per cent were fought chiefly for wages and hours. (The balance were "miscellaneous.") Up through 1926, indeed, the organization issue never represented twenty-five per cent of the total. Thereafter there was an abrupt rise, stimulated partly by the general prosperity and by 1929 about forty per cent of the strikes were fought for collective bargaining. Then, after declining during the depression, the curve proceeded upward, breaking through forty per cent in 1934, and reaching fifty per cent in 1936 and fifty-three per cent for the first half of this year—which so far as the record goes is an all-time high. This can be expressed in another way. In the fourteen-year period beginning with 1919 there were in round numbers 20,000 strikes. Of these, 5,000 were primarily for union recognition. But in four years beginning with 1933 there were some 7,000 strikes. Of these, 3,000 were primarily for union recognition.

"Strike"

The fact that half of the 1936 strikes were fought for a principle, with the trend continuing into the stormy spring and summer of 1937, is of such significance that those who follow labor closely are inclined to doubt the comfortable theory, . . . to the effect that the current wave of strikes is just a normal postdepression phenomenon. Coupled with the prodigious growth of union membership, the increased percentage of strikes won and compromised, and the apparent trend toward quicker settlements, it would seem to indicate the recrudescence of a major mass movement with its roots far in the American past. One must, to be sure, make allowances for Roosevelt "prosperity," which has made it possible for the worker to afford to fight for principles. And one must make a big allowance for assistance rendered by the government. This latter element, however, is itself symptomatic of a real pressure, for the machinery of Washington, unpredictable as its motion may be, does not operate in a vacuum of pure idealism. Washington has strengthened labor's position, not just for the hell of it, but in response to forces that the depression stimulated and revitalized.

So much, at any rate, the realist must admit. It is useless in a situation such as this to hide one's head in the sand—to suppose, as some employers do, that labor's recent drive has been stopped. It may be that the lull in big strikes will continue for some time. But it is possible that even if it does— and even if the violent manifestations of labor's unrest are somehow avoided—labor is in a position to consolidate and even increase its new gains. It has the machinery, whether for peace or for war. And it is rapidly acquiring the men. . . .

As already stated, the modern phase of the labor movement, the post-NRA phase, represents a distinct evolution, and the progress of the evolution has been fraught with warfare of the most harrowing character. It is of course impossible to choose from the 10,000 strikes included in this phase any several that would give a complete evolutionary picture; but it is possible to choose a few strikes to illustrate the more important points. . . . They are presented herewith.

TEXTILES, 1934

Mushroom Unions

If you were a union worker in the southern cotton textile industry on September 1, 1934, your earnings were around $11 a week—and in general you could expect a wage of little more than half the national average for workers in manufacturing. You probably lived in a town of less than 10,000 people. Unlike the 100,000 weavers, spinners, loom fixers, card grinders, smash hands, slubber tenders, and other cotton textile workers of the North, you lived in a region where the traditions of organized labor were not strong. You were new to industry, and there was much you disliked about it. Your great complaint was what you called the stretch-out, for if, under the NRA cotton textile code, you worked a basic forty-hour week, you insisted that you produced more than formerly in fifty hours. For instance, you used to make 144 dozen bloomers in ten hours, but now in eight hours you turned out 200 dozen bloomers. You might complain of "docks," of fines, of cases where a week's work brought in $5.88. You were one unit in a vast, disorderly, depressed industry, made up of some 1,200 mills operated by some 850 companies. And, you were probably in a union for the first time in your life.

More immediately, since June your position had grown worse. In that month the cotton textile code authority had reduced production twenty five per cent, which meant a sharp cut in your wages. There was a state-wide textile strike in Alabama. The delegates of your local, meeting at the national convention of the United Textile Workers in August, had voted for an industry-wide strike, demanding a thirty-hour week with no wage reduction, more uniform wages in the North and South, establishment of maximum work loads, reinstatement of workers fired for union membership, and—which has most bearing on this article—recognition of the union. Francis Gorman, Fifth Vice President of the Union, had sent the demands to George Arthur Sloan, President of the Cotton Textile Institute and Chairman of the Cotton Textile Code Authority. He replied that no one could bargain for the entire industry and that the strike was a strike against the code. And the cotton textile code was no ordinary code. The first of all NRA codes, under which average hourly wages increased sixty-five per cent in a year, it outlawed child labor, established a labor board to handle disputes, and was generally regarded as one of the most liberal, as Sloan himself was judged a liberal trade association head. But the union charged that 2,000 cases brought before the board brought no appreciable results. And after six weeks, on September 1, 1934, at 11:30 P.M., you, as a good union man, went on strike.

You were caught up, in fact, in the first surge of the strike wave already described in statistics—and your strike accounted for almost 400,000 of the 1,467,000 workers who were involved that year. Above all, it was a strike of a union that had increased its members enormously under the impetus of the NRA drive, the United Textile Workers having grown from some 15,000 before the NRA to claim 300,000 in cotton textiles alone.

The textile strike was a strike involving primarily workers new to organized labor, pitted against a bitterly depressed industry, which meant that it was violent and brief. Twelve strikers and one deputy were killed in the three weeks that it raged. It was also emotional. "God is with us," cried a southern organizer as the strike began, "He will not desert us in this just struggle for ourselves and our families." It was characterized by what liberal economists politely call "employer resistance to collective bargaining." "Mobs of hoodlums and thugs!" thundered the President of the Alabama Manufacturers' Association, after a clash in the mill town of Boaz, "producing something like civil war in the South!" And the New England trade journal *Fibre and Fabric* asserted: "A few hundred funerals will have a quieting influence." The strike was followed by a period of disillusionment with section 7A and the elaborate mediation apparatus of the New Deal. With consequences that will presently be examined.

Largely because of its mushroom growth, the union could not support a long-drawn-out struggle. Facing enormous expenses, it had less than $1,000,000 in the treasury, and the strike might involve 500,000 cotton textile workers—to say nothing of about 700,000 other workers in silk, wool, rayon, and other branches of the industry. It had four regional offices covering thirteen states and seventy organizers. When Gorman handed out his orders for simultaneous transmission to 500 locals of the unions, he knew that the strike could not last longer than three weeks—or, as time is measured during strikes, he had 500 hours in which to win or lose.

The picket lines of fresh recruits tightened around hundreds of the industry's mills, and they stopped production so effectively that textile trade papers reported, along with indignant accounts of violence, that the employers felt they had been outgeneraled by an "audacious and intelligent minority." In the South, during the first week of the strike, fifty flying squadrons of pickets, with from 200 to 650 men in each column of cars, were operating along a 110-mile front from Gastonia to Greenville in the Carolinas. At Trion, Georgia, a deputy sheriff, a picket, and a strike sympathizer were killed and fifteen strikers were wounded in a two-hour pitched battle; at Greenville another strike sympathizer was killed, and during the strike's course there were clashes between pickets, deputies, nonstrikers, and Guardsmen as far afield as Woonsocket, Rhode Island, Lancaster, Pennsylvania, and Augusta, Georgia, where three more strikers were shot, one fatally. At the gate of the Chiquola Manufacturing Company's plant at Honea Path, South Carolina, a group of armed men opposing the strike charged the picket line, firing, killing six pickets and wounding fifteen. The union said that the armed group were deputies; the employers said they were nonstriking workers. By the second week of the strike more than 15,000 National Guardsmen had been mobilized in seven states, and a concentration camp for pickets had been set up in Georgia.

The strike's violence created so much bitter controversy that its fundamental issues were obscured. The union's introduction of flying squadrons of pickets, a then relatively unfamiliar weapon that it took over from the coal miners, caused a furor in the press. The employers claimed that the use of these groups of strikers in automobiles, descending on towns suddenly and unexpectedly, was proof that the union had the support of only a minority of the employees in each plant.

For this charge the union's rejoinder ran roughly as follows: the employees in company towns, especially in the South, could not form picket lines because of armed guards employed by the companies. Nor could ordinary organizing procedure be followed. At Rockmart, Georgia, the president of the local was kidnaped and driven from town; at Winfield, Alabama, two union officials were caught by thirty-three armed guards of the Alabama Mills Company and ordered to leave the county. And so forth. Against such odds, the union said, the only way a picket line could be established was by means of a flying squadron. At Fitchburg, Massachusetts, for instance, Organizer Powers Hapgood led fifty pickets to the edge of town, but was turned back by police. Later he returned with a flying squadron of 500 recruits drawn from a number of striking mills and succeeded in establishing a picket line. Whereupon the plant in Fitchburg also came out.

But underlying this was the matter of a union with limited resources and a vastly increased membership, waging a strike over an enormous area and around hundreds of mills, unevenly organized within the industry, with inexperienced strikers to man its picket lines—picket lines, the union asserts, that were attacked with forces strong enough to demoralize the most seasoned of hard-bitten unionists. And when the Winant Board issued a report that was a moral victory for the textile workers (since it recognized their basic grievances as real) but was a practical defeat (since it made no provisions for immediate or specific relief), the union called the strike off. "The union has won an overwhelming victory," said Gorman, the union complaining three weeks later that 25,000 strikers had been blacklisted. By the next year the membership claim of the United Textile Workers declined by about two-thirds.

Thus, if you were an average textile worker who went on strike on September 1, 1934, you probably came out of it three weeks later burdened with considerable doubt as to the effectiveness of section 7A. You had been a part of a mushroom growth of unionism that came into being with the signing of the NRA and fell away soon after.

REMINGTON RAND: 1936

The Back-to-Work Movement Develops

If you were an aligner, say, in Remington Rand's ancient red brick Ilion plant your union experiences were of a far more complex character. As an aligner you were one of the most skilled workers in the complicated field of typewriter and business machine manufacture, but during the depression you may have earned as little as $350 a year, and girls in the factory got as little as sixteen cents an hour. You probably owned your own home in Ilion, but it was mortgaged. In 1933, soon after the NRA was signed and while the textile workers were being organized, a federal union was chartered in the factory, the old craft unions expanded, and by intricate steps too numerous to be traced here, you presently found yourself in John Frey's Metal Trades Department of the A.F. of L., organized, along with the employees of the four— later six—Remington Rand plants, into a Joint Protective Board of Office Equipment Workers.

Your union went through some of the typical troubles of the new unions of that period. Mr. Rand would not recognize it as exclusive bargaining agent, and on May 9, 1934, you went on strike. After five weeks, the union was recognized as a bargaining agency for its members (it claimed ninety per cent of the production and maintenance workers).

But the troubles of your union were only beginning. Through the winter of 1936, as a good union man, you were worried at rumors that Remington Rand had bought a huge abandoned automobile factory at Elmira, New York, and planned to move operations there, developing a new typewriter known as the Madame X. The union was worried because of the contract with Rand, covering the employees of six Rand factories. Would the contract apply in the new Elmira plant? And was the plant at Ilion to close? With these questions agitating them, union officials tried to see Rand. They charged, and the Labor Board later upheld them, that Rand's refusal to see them was a violation of their right of collective bargaining. To the company their questions were an unwarranted intrusion into management and an attempt to find out plans that could not be announced without disclosures to competitors. Plant managers conferred with union people discussing other matters of the contract, but could give no satisfactory answer to the crucial question of what was going to happen at Elmira with Madame X. For these and other reasons a strike vote was taken on April 28, and by a vote of 3,200 to 568, union officers were empowered to call a strike if, in their opinion, "all other means have failed to bring about a satisfactory conclusion."

The union contract contained a confidential clause. It read: "It is understood and agreed that any discrimination or intimidation on the part of any employee toward any other employee shall be just cause for discharge." As the union understood it, this only confirmed the public clause of the contract, which pledged both parties to the maintenance of peace and harmony—"We were not to bother or harm the few scabs, and they were to keep their skirts clean," was the union's interpretation. But on May 21, three weeks after the union authorized the strike, this confidential agreement became the mainspring of action. All employees of Remington Rand had received ballots distributed by the management, reading: *Are you dissatisfied with present working conditions? Are you in favor of a strike?* In the Syracuse plant the union leaders stopped work until the balloting was called off. Whereupon the company closed the plant for two weeks. Rand informed the mayor that he would re-open after the sixteen union leaders had been discharged—the point being, he insisted, that they had violated the confidential agreement in preventing the balloting. In Ilion, Syracuse, Tonawanda, Middletown, and Norwood, the union prepared for a strike, sending a last wire asking Rand if he was not letting "anger instead of reason rule." There was no reply. The second Remington Rand strike began.

If you were a good union man in Ilion you probably went to the strike meeting at the Temple Theatre on the night of May 25, listened to the speeches and turned out on the picket line the next morning. You may have eaten a sandwich at strike headquarters nearby. You may have watched the thirty-odd newly hired guards of Foster's Detective Bureau arriving to patrol the plant interior. And then things began to happen—not only to you, but to the mayor, the chief of police, a number of small city businessmen, the employees of Remington Rand in other cities, and a number of professional guards. In Ilion a Citizens' Committee was started by Barney Allen, Ilion's retail dealer in General Electric supplies. He was afraid Remington Rand would move out of Ilion, taking the $12,000-a-day payroll that was the town's main income. An organization called the Ilion Typewriter Employees' Protective Association was started by Reginald Boote, a young aligner who opposed the strike. It opened an office and began signing up employees who wanted to go back to work. A "For Sale" sign appeared on the factory. There was one tense moment the second day, with a threatened riot arising out of a brief encounter between strikers and guards. The Citizens' Committee appealed to Governor Lehman to send state troopers to supplement Ilion's six regular officers. He refused, since there had been no violence. Failing, the Citizens' Committee demanded that the mayor appoint 300 special deputies. In an atmosphere of growing hysteria, the Citizens' Committee held a mass meeting; Barney Allen called upon the mayor to co-operate or resign; the mayor agreed to co-operate (but he refused to ring the fire bell to summon the volunteer firemen to be deputized); and 300 deputies were signed up.

On the morning of June 10 the streets near the plant were roped off. Tear gas guns were mounted in the factory windows. Across the street members of Reginald Boote's Ilion Typewriter Employees' Association gathered for an open meeting. There were a few skirmishes between strikers and nonstrikers, ending when tear gas bombs were fired. Then the members and sympathizers of the Ilion Typewriter Employees' Protective Association (500 says the union, 800 says Reginald Boote) entered the factory; the flag rose on the factory flagpole; the "For Sale" sign was taken down; and Rand arrived to address the returning employees. That night a state of emergency was declared in Ilion on the strength of rumors that a flying squadron of strikers from Syracuse was rushing to town to help the Ilion pickets. All roads were blocked. The union headquarters were padlocked. During the "siege of Ilion," as the strikers called it, Union Leader Harold Beer (who had worked for Remington Rand for twenty-five years) entered Ilion by going on foot through the woods that lie behind the town. And the siege ended when the strikers broke, more than 1,200 returning to work two days after the strike began.

If you were a union man in Remington Rand's Ilion plant in 1936 you were one atom in the working out of a new force, which, amid charges and countercharges, accusations of prejudice, partisanship, plotting, and worse, was to be analyzed and defined by the National Labor Relations Board as the Mohawk Valley Formula. The nine steps of the Mohawk Valley Formula it found to include: (1) conducting a forced balloting under the direction of foremen to misrepresent the strength of the union, calling strike leaders "agitators," forming a Citizens' Committee under threat to move the plant; (2) arousing the community by calling for "law and order" because of "wholly imagined violence"; (3) calling mass meetings of citizens; (4) calling for armed deputies; (5) starting a back-to-work movement; (6) setting a date for opening the plant; (7) staging the opening theatrically; (8) turning the "locality into a warlike camp"; (9) keeping up a campaign of publicity to convince the remaining strikers that the plant is in full operation.

Thus the Labor Board pictured Rand as a superstrategist of strikebreaking and the originator of a foolproof strikebreaking technique. It revealed that during the Remington Rand strike the company paid, in all, $25,800 to Pearl L. Bergoff for his services and the services of 200 guards and "missionaries," whose function it was to discourage the strikers, $30,000 more to Captain Foster of Foster's Industrial and

Detective Bureau, and an additional $25,000 to Raymond J. Burns of the William J. Burns International Detective Agency, Inc., the latter two, according to the company, for protection because of the recurring violence of the strike, which in some of its six towns lasted longer and was more bitterly fought than at Ilion. The Labor Board found Rand guilty of unfair labor practices and ordered him to offer reinstatement to all strikers unemployed, the case going to the courts, where it still remains. The Joint Committee of Remington Rand Employees' Associations (the Board called the one at Ilion "a puppet association . . . secretly organized by the employer") denounced the Board and said its conclusions were based on the false statements of disgruntled ex-employees. And Remington Rand, which had not called witnesses at the Labor Board hearings, called the Board's charges a slander.

In the history of the Wagner Act, and in the Remington Rand strike itself, these charges and countercharges are of primary significance. But in the wave of 10,000 strikes, of which the Remington Rand strike was only a part, they are of less importance than the trends the strike revealed. For the Remington Rand strike shows quite clearly what other strikes barely suggest—the mechanics of a modern back-to-work movement.

RUBBER, 1936

The Sitdown Begins

Some observer poised high above the class struggle about that time might have thought that capital now had all the advantage, with labor's enthusiasm for the NRA ended and the spectacular, co-ordinated, theatrical Mohawk Valley Formula presently to come into being as an instrument for breaking strikes almost as soon as they got under way. And it might have seemed that with some of the mushroom unions of the NRA period smashed in their attempt to achieve recognition (as in the textile industry) and others broken after they had achieved it (as in the Remington Rand strike), the strike wave was now due to shrink to the proportions of an episode in labor's uneven history.

Instead, out in Akron, Ohio, at three in the morning of February 14, 1936, something happened that sent the strike wave surging to a new high—although its results were not immediately apparent. A major strike began in the rubber industry, growing out of a tangle of accumulated grievances, but taking a form that gave it historical importance. The form it took may have been a natural development in a long chain of brief stay-in and slow-down strikes. But whatever the reason, on that night a group of tire builders in Goodyear Tire & Rubber Company's Plant II sat down on the job. Theirs was not the first sitdown. But theirs grew into the Goodyear rubber strike that lasted five weeks, involved 14,000 employees, saw an eleven-mile picket line, and was described by the Department of Labor as "characterized by a lack of violence." It gave the sitdown nationwide publicity, ended with partial recognition of the union, and launched a drive that swept Akron's rubber union membership from less than 2,000 to approximately 37,000, the United Rubber Workers of America from about 3,000 to an organization of 75,000 with 136 locals and the reputation of never having lost a strike.

But it did not begin impressively. On that stormy St. Valentine's Day in Akron, Goodyear's management distributed some unwelcome valentines to sixty-nine tire builders of Plant II—the pink slips that meant a layoff. (February sales had been bad, said the management.) The first three men who got them, according to the story, "swore and sat down." They and many others remained sitting down while production heads hurried to the factory. The later shifts coming to work elected committees to support them, and—most important—the conveyers leading to the department were filled and the hot and steamy curing department immediately beyond had no tires to prepare. At nine in the morning the first sitdowners left the plant. Later shifts intermittently worked and sat down. At nine-forty that night Goodyear's outraged management gave notice that anyone not back at work in forty minutes would be dropped from the payroll. At ten-thirty the foremen began handing out notices. One hundred and thirty-seven men were dismissed. Thereafter the progress of the strike became confused—over the issues involved (it grew out of the union's opposition to increased hours and the threat of a wage cut); over union politics (since the union was one of the mushroom unions of the A.F. of L. involved in the split with the C.I.O.); over a back-to-work movement that flourished briefly and died; and over the numerous settlements proposed to end the strike. In the rubber strike itself, in Akron politics, and in the struggle between the A. F. of L. and the C.I.O., these subtleties were of first importance. But in the wave of strikes the sitdowns in Goodyear rubber were consequential because they introduced one of labor's answers to the Mohawk Valley Formula or the less highly organized back-to-work movements of the other side. In the auto strikes that came soon after the sitdown it was to make history on a grand scale. And in the strike in Little Steel, the Mohawk Valley Formula was (perhaps) to be applied on a scale no less sweeping.

AUTOS, 1936-37

The Sitdown

By November, 1936, the strike wave we have been describing had added up to over 7,000 strikes. It had included at least six general strikes, the great maritime strikes of the East and West Coast, a nationwide miners' strike, and a multitude of small strikes that followed in the wake of the big ones. It had passed through two distinct stages, suggested by our accounts of the textile strike and the strike at Remington Rand. And it looked as if it were going to decline. The number of strikes had increased slightly through 1936 but the number of men involved had gone down—which meant that the strike wave was now reaching smaller plants, and the figures were swollen by the inclusion of later strikes, strikes of grocery clerks, even by a strike of the graveyard workers of Minneapolis.

Then—to set an arbitrary date for the beginning of the next surge—at eight-twenty-five on the sunny morning of November 18, 1936, five men in the trim department of General Motors' Fisher Body plant in Atlanta were laid off because they came to work wearing union buttons. To General Motors that was a violation of company rules. To the union their dismissal was part of a general attempt to smash the United Automobile Workers, and a sitdown strike occurred. If you were a member of the union and had observed it rise and fall, you probably believed that the systematic firing of union men was part of General Motors policy. You may have joined the auto workers union in 1934 when, as a skyrocketing federal union of the A.F. of L., it claimed 200,000, with 60,000 members in Detroit. You may have been with it in 1935 when it plummeted down to the point where William Green could complain: "Today, I am sorry to say, we have 35,000. A year ago there were more, but for different reasons they are not with us now." Among those reasons was one later revealed by the La Follette Committee: that General Motors had spent $839,000 in two and a half years on detective services, that a Lansing local had five members, all officers and all stool pigeons provided by a spy agency hired by the company.

If you were a rank-and-file union man among General Motors' 135,000 employees, your biggest grievance was the "speedup"—the most likely cause for a "conflagration in the automobile industry," the NRA's Research and Planning Division had reported. And as a union man, the subsequent months of that conflagration were the most important of your union experience. There was a strike at the Kansas City Fisher Body plant when a union man was fired for jumping over the assembly line. There were three sitdown strikes in the auto-parts industry: at Bendix in South Bend and at Midland Steel and Kelsey-Hayes in Detroit. In Cleveland and Norwood, Ohio, there were General Motors walkouts; at the General Motors Guide Lamp Plant in Anderson, Indiana, there was a sitdown involving 2,400; and in the long, rectangular, brick factories that house the Fisher Body plants of Flint, the strike was touching the heart of the General Motors empire.

Deep in the interior of Fisher I, about a mile away from the imposing group of factories in the central General Motors plant, a sitdown started on December 30. The union had presented a contract to the company a few days before, and now the strikers saw (or thought they saw, for the the big dies from which turret-top bodies are made. Which, they assumed, company says it never happened) preparations being made for removing must mean that the plant was being abandoned. Or that a scare was being thrown into Flint, 45,000 of whose 150,000 work for General Motors. At Fisher II, across Chevrolet Avenue from Chevrolet II, three inspectors who were union men were demoted to the assembly line. (Because they were union men, said the union; because they were supervisors, said the company, and supervisors could not belong to the union.) Workers sat down in both Fisher plants. During the rubber strike, the sitdowners left the plant, formed their picket lines outside. But at Flint several hundred strikers remained in Fisher I and II. The union listed eight demands, including a thirty-hour week, seniority rights, a national agreement, and joint determination of the speed of the line. The company replied that the plants had to be vacated before there could be any discussion. The stage was set for what motor makers still call Detroit's sociological nightmare.

Seen only in relation to Detroit, or to the state of Michigan (where for a period one person in every thirty-three was on strike), or to the automobile industry, the sitdown certainly assumed nightmarish proportions. And because during the General Motors strike there was dancing twenty-four hours a day in Flint at the strike headquarters at Pengelly Hall, plus ball games in the struck plants, plus food prepared for the strikers by a union chef formerly of Detroit's swank Athletic Club, the sitdowns seemed to take place in a nightmare world where the laws of capitalism, if they operated at all, worked the way the laws of gravity do in a dream. But if viewed in relation to the 1933-37 strike wave, the General Motors strike becomes part of a great pattern. It saw, for example, a back-to-work movement, as well as an injunction against the strikers. The injunction was defied, and the back-to-work movement collapsed, for reasons connected not only with the sitdown, but with the change in labor's tactics in general.

During the strike General Motors got an injunction to evict the sitdowners. But the injunction lost some of its authority when the union promptly disclosed that Judge Edward Black, who issued it, owned 1,000 shares of General Motors stock. Whereupon General Motors got another injunction from another judge. But the sheriff who went inside the plant to read it to the strikers was greeted with boos and catcalls. And Governor Murphy refused to order the National Guard to enforce the injunction until all peaceful means of settlement had been exhausted.

As for the back-to-work movement, in this case called the "Flint Alliance for Security of Our Jobs, Our Homes, and Our Community," it came to its own peculiar kind of grief. While it was growing to claim 12,000 and making preparations for a mass meeting, Governor Murphy was holding conferences with General Motors and the union. On January 11 there was an unexpected crisis: the sitdowners remaining in Fisher II thought an attempt was going to be made to evict them. Heat was cut down; the company guards who had previously handed food into the factory now refused to let it enter. But according to General Motors the strikers had for the first time prevented the office force from going to work, which was why the heat was turned off, and although the company guards would no longer hand food into the plant, they would permit it to be handed through the windows. Whatever the reason, the situation suddenly became ominous. By nightfall police had assembled around the plant. In the beginning of a battle that lasted for seven hours, the police broke a window in the plant and fired a tear gas shell inside; the strikers built a barricade of autos in the street, doused the tear gas bombs with water from a fire hose, and held their ground. On the third rush the police fired, and fourteen strikers were wounded. And the next day militia massed at Flint, the Fleetwood plant went on strike, while from Washington John Lewis announced that the auto strikers would have the full support of the C.I.O. and Homer Martin hurried to Washington to confer with him.

During the forty-eight crowded hours after the riot in Flint, the ascetic Governor Murphy (whose picture, labeled "Our Friend," looked sternly down on several hundred sitdowners) arranged the famous "Lansing Truce." By its terms the union agreed to evacuate the plants, General Motors agreed not to resume operations in the struck plants, and the union temporarily waived its sole bargaining demand. So it came about that on Saturday, January 16, the sitdowners left the Guide Lamp plant in Anderson, Cadillac and Fleetwood in Detroit. But in Flint a hitch occurred. Talkative ex-Mayor George Boysen, once a Buick paymaster, organizer of the Flint Alliance, told a reporter that at four o'clock Sunday afternoon General Motors would announce that it was going to deal with the Alliance. The sitdowners were scheduled to leave the plants at one o'clock. Informed of this, the union refused to evacuate Fisher I and Fisher II in Flint, and the General Motors strike flared up again.

Such happenings gave a good share of Michigan's population its conviction that law and order had collapsed. But seen in perspective against the strike wave, they illustrated how profoundly union tactics, as well as unions themselves, had changed in the period since the textile strike.

Unlike the Remington Rand strikers, the auto strikers had successfully countered a back-to-work movement. They had developed a new organizing technique and a new strike strategy. But more profoundly, they had developed a new concept of strike action, which is nowhere better illustrated than in the story of the seizure of Chevvy IV. By the end of the first month of the strike union leaders wanted a bold stroke to bolster union morale. Half a dozen of them went to the bluff overlooking the seven plants on Chevrolet's eighty-acre tract and decided that they had to capture Plant IV, which assembles motors for all Chevrolet automobiles. If the union could get and hold that plant, they could give General Motors all the rest of its establishment and still stop enough production to count.

But a direct attack on Chevvy IV was out of the question. Hardly a hundred feet from this plant was the personnel building, which served as the headquarters and arsenal for the company police. It was too well guarded. Furthermore, the union was not very strong there. They decided to make a false attempt to take Chevrolet IX, a bearing plant on the other end of the tract. Not more than eight strike leaders knew the full details of the plan.

First, thirty-five shop stewards were called to a meeting. It was held after midnight in Fisher I, where the sitdown was in progress, to impress them with its importance and secrecy. Among them, by design, were men known by the organizers to be informers. They were told that an effort would be made to capture Chevrolet IX. This plan met with strong objection because the men knew that the bearing plant would be hard to take—and also that it was relatively unimportant to production because General Motors could get bearings elsewhere. Nevertheless, the program was decided on.

At 3:00 P.M. on February 1, a mass meeting was held in Pengelly Hall. At 3:20 a note was handed up to Bob Travis, chairman of the meeting, who then announced that there was trouble at Chevrolet IX and that everybody should go down there at once. Actually, nothing had yet happened at Chevrolet IX, but promptly at 3:30 at the change of shift the men refused to work, refused to leave the plant, and set up a terrific din. When the strikers from Pengelly Hall arrived at 3:35 the "trouble" at Chevrolet IX was in progress.

As had been expected, guards rushed to the plant. Meanwhile, at Chevrolet VI, far from the scene of the trouble, promptly at 3:35 a union steward named Ed Cronk sounded a siren, picked up an American flag, and started marching around the factory. He led the march to Chevrolet IV. But in his excitement he forgot to look around, discovering when he got to Chevrolet IV that he had only twenty-five men with him. He rushed back and marched around the factory again, carrying the flag, and this time collected more followers. Once in Chevvy IV the strikers quickly ejected foremen, plant officials, and nonunion workers and began to barricade all the doors. Fourteen minutes had elapsed between the time the commotion had started at Chevrolet IX and the time Chevrolet IV was barricaded.

Out of all the sensational news of the auto strike, the seizing of Chevvy IV was the high point. In terms of the auto strike alone it was either the final indignity offered outraged property rights—if you were on the side of the employers—or an illustration of labor's growing initiative—if you were not. But in terms of the 1933-37 strike wave its significance is of a different order. When you compare it with the moves made during the textile strike it serves as a landmark, measuring how far labor had traveled in less than three years and through some 4,000 strikes.

BIG STEEL, LITTLE STEEL: RECOGNITION AND CONFLICT

*Manifesto: American Iron and Steel Institute (1936) ***

TO THE PUBLIC AND THE EMPLOYEES
IN THE STEEL INDUSTRY

A campaign to unionize the employees of the Steel Industry has been announced.

In order that the employees and the public may know the position of the Steel Industry in the face of the threatened drive, the Industry makes this statement through the American Iron and Steel Institute.

Persons and organizations not connected with the Industry have taken charge of the campaign.

There are many disturbing indications that the promoters of the campaign will employ coercion and intimidation of the employees in the Industry and foment strikes.

The objective of the campaign is the "closed shop," which prohibits the employment of any one not a union member. The Steel Industry will oppose any attempt to compel its employees to join a union or to pay tribute for the right to work.

No employee in the steel industry has to join any organization to get or hold a job. Employment in the Industry does not depend upon membership or nonmembership in any organization. Advancement depends on

* The Manifesto, June 29, 1936. Reprinted in *Fortune*, XV (May 1937), 91.

individual merit and effort. These are fundamental American principles to which the Industry will steadfastly adhere.

The Steel Industry believes in the principles of collective bargaining, and it is in effect throughout the Industry.

The overwhelming majority of the employees in the Steel Industry recently participated in annual elections under their own representation plans and elected their representatives for collective bargaining. The elections were conducted by the employees themselves by secret ballot. One of the purposes of an announced campaign is to overthrow those plans and the representatives so elected.

The Steel Industry is recovering from six years of depression and huge losses, and the employees are now beginning to receive the benefits of increased operations. Any interruption of the forward movement will seriously injure the employees and their families and all businesses dependent upon the Industry, and will endanger the welfare of the country.

The announced drive, with its accompanying agitation for industrial strife, threatens such interruption.

The Steel Industry will use its resources to the best of its ability to protect its employees and their families from intimidation, coercion, and violence and to aid them in maintaining collective bargaining free from interference from any source.

"It Happened in Steel" (1937) *

On June 27, 1936, Myron Charles Taylor, Chairman of the Board of U.S. Steel Corp., set sail for Europe. This was no unusual move for him, for besides his obvious interest in international affairs he owns a former Medici property outside of Florence and he likes to wander solemnly through museums and cathedrals. But Mr. Taylor sailed for Europe in 1936 in a peculiarly philosophical mood. Lesser men than he could see the handwriting that John Llewellyn Lewis had written on the forbidding walls of the Corporation's mills. It was evident to Mr. Taylor that a great change had come over the face of United States industry. The blood and brimstone labor philosophy of his predecessor, Judge Elbert H. Gary, was out of tune with the times. So was the covering material under which the Judge had sought to hide its worst horrors (perhaps even from himself); the idea of the big steel "family," for instance, and good will toward the worker, and social welfare. Labor was in arms. What *Fortune* later described (in October) as "the ir-

* From "It Happened in Steel," *Fortune*, XV (May 1937), 91-94, 176, 179-180. Copyright 1937 by Time Inc. Reprinted by special permission.

repressible conflict of the twentieth century" had broken out. The industrial problem had become a social problem, and unless something were done about it, the social problem would presently generate chaos.

But what was to be done? To give in to labor spinelessly meant to lose control over the business one had been hired to manage. To fight labor adamantly meant, for a long time, no business at all. In its unhurried course Mr. Taylor's mind explored the various angles—possible, probable, past, and future. And after he had reached the ancient enclosure of his Florentine villa he felt that he had made enough progress to sit down and write himself a memorandum. This he did. He wrote it and tore it up and rewrote it and revised it and rewrote it again. And at length there emerged a dozen crystal lines, remarkable not so much for the originality of their substance as for their unambiguous expression of a fundamental compromise. So terse were those lines that they cannot properly be defined as a memorandum. They constitute a formula—the Myron Taylor formula for industrial peace. Hitherto this document has been known only to a limited circle of friends, to whom Mr. Taylor showed it when he returned to the United States. But a few copies do exist outside of Mr. Taylor's private file. And this is what they say:

> The Company recognizes the right of its employees to bargain collectively through representatives freely chosen by them without dictation, coercion, or intimidation in any form or from any source. It will negotiate and contract with the representatives of any group of its employees so chosen and with any organization as the representative of its members, subject to the recognition of the principle that the right to work is not dependent on membership or nonmembership in any organization and subject to the right of every employee freely to bargain in such manner and through such representatives, if any, as he chooses.

That was all. Whether by coincidence or design, the statement is exactly one hundred words long, and these one hundred words represent a summer's work. But they packed more dynamite than any one hundred words ever written by a United States industrialist. Superficially they inject no new principle, and hence do not shriek from the housetops. Fundamentally, however, they bring forth and formulate what was previously only inchoate; and in this sense they achieve the dignity of statesmanship. For reasons best known to himself, Mr. Taylor never gave these words to the world. As a result of his reticence no one outside of his most intimate acquaintances has understood what the Chairman has been up to. The greatest news story of the day—his settlement on March 1, 1937, with John L. Lewis and the C.I.O.—followed logically from the formula and incorporated its every point. But since no one has known about the formula, no one has been able to explain that spectacular event.

A body of rumor and legend has therefore grown up around the Taylor-Lewis agreement, and the process has been encouraged by the fact that the two men worked in the most incredible secrecy. The nation's most potent industrialist and the nation's most dramatic laborite, the latter making front-page news almost every day in the General Motors strike, succeeded in meeting each other ten or twelve times during a period of fifty days without arousing the suspicions of the most alert newshawks in the world. But the real story is neither complicated nor mysterious. Shorn of analysis and of a few intimate passages that must await the publication of somebody's memoirs, it goes like this.

Shortly after one o'clock, in the big dining room of Washington's Mayflower Hotel, the business of eating lunch was halted. There had entered the room at that moment a tall and austere man and a handsome woman, known to most persons present as Mr. and Mrs. Myron C. Taylor. But as Mr. and Mrs. Taylor advanced, who should be seated in their path, halfway through lunch, but Pennsylvania's Senator Joseph F. Guffey and C.I.O.'s rugged Chairman, John L. Lewis. As he passed this pair of laborites, Mr. Taylor bowed. And having seated his wife at a nearby table, he conspicuously returned to Senator Guffey's table, where he held out his hand, first to the Senator and next to Mr. Lewis. The three men then stood chatting for almost a minute, whereupon Mr. Taylor, having delivered himself of a pleasantry, turned and rejoined his wife.

If the Mayflower dining room had not been the nation's No. 1 meeting place frequented by political sophisticates, the shock of this encounter might not have been so general; but as it was, both the waiters and the luncheoners lost all interest in lunch. Moreover, the poise of the room was broken all over again some minutes later when Senator Guffey and Mr. Lewis finished eating. This pair now crossed over to Mr. Taylor's table, where they greeted Mrs. Taylor, Mr. Lewis meeting her for the first time. Senator Guffey then hurried on; but the inspirator of the C.I.O. sat down and remained seated for more than twenty minutes, carrying on an animated conversation with his host and hostess (which no one could overhear) and calling forth frequent bursts of laughter.

That was on Saturday, January 9, 1937. Though no one in the room heard him say it, Mr. Lewis remarked to Mr. Taylor that he would like a meeting with him sometime in the near future. And Mr. Taylor at once suggested the next day. The next day was Sunday, a day on which Mr. Lewis never talks business; but this matter was apparently so important that he acquiesced, and after some little palaver it was decided

that Mr. Taylor's suite in the Mayflower would make the least conspicuous rendezvous. . . .

The Chairman was confronted with a problem in metamorphosis. The
metamorphosis, to be sure, was never at any time so violent as some
people like to suppose. To begin with, when the traditional labor policy
of the Corporation is boiled down to its essentials it is seen to consist in
the theory of little more than an insistence upon the open shop. Here
and there the Corporation has had dealings with unions. For many years
it has been constrained to recognize the United Mine Workers in the
state of Illinois—a situation which has not worked badly. And other
contracts have been made with the U.M.W.A. in recent times, notably
those concerning the captive mines. But the trouble with the Corporation's
labor policy was that, in practice, it *over*defended the open shop, resorting
to the most violent methods of labor warfare, including the late Coal and
Iron Police, state troops, local cops, and spies.[1] In this way it earned
its reputation of being, not the champion of the open shop, but the enemy
of all organized labor. The lurid atmosphere thus created was also
breathed by the independents, some of which were even more aggressive
than big steel. And the result was incipient war. On June 29 last, when the
industry (including the Corporation) issued the [antiunion] proclamation
through the American Iron and Steel Institute [see previous selection],
the war was actually declared. For that proclamation was directed
squarely at John L. Lewis, against whom it sought to set up the company-
union system.

Now Mr. Taylor, as we have seen, sailed for Europe on June 27, two
days before this manifesto appeared. Just before he sailed he had gone
on record against it—not strongly enough to stop it, certainly, but
nevertheless on record to some of his associates. And he did strenuously
oppose the Institute's subsequent move, by which it published the
manifesto as an advertisement in leading newspapers at a cost of some
$150,000. Which leads to some interesting points. Mr. Taylor is a dif-
ferent sort of man from Judge Gary or anyone else who has ever had an
important position in steel. He is not a steel man and hence is not particularly fascinated with the traditions of the steel country. And after
his own deliberate fashion, he is a liberal. Mr. Taylor's liberalism is not
of any standard variety. The Chairman is perhaps the closest thing in the
United States to a British Conservative—a man who, having measured
the strength of a progressive adversary, has the foresight to anticipate
him. The United States steel industry as a whole, on the other hand, is
characterized by conservatives of another stripe. Most of them would

[1] Mr. Taylor sent out an order liquidating U.S. Steel's spy system two
years ago, but ambitious underlings have clung to the practice nevertheless.

rather be damned than give in to the Left. Mr. Taylor played along with them for years, and then, in the course of fifty days, simply decided not to.

Two facts support the contention that Mr. Taylor is a United States model of a British Conservative. The first takes us back to the time when he bumped into Mr. Lewis in the coal strike of 1933. Of the 16,000 men employed in the Corporation's captive mines Mr. Lewis then controlled only about 4,000, but in spite of this fact he was holding out for a closed shop and exclusive bargaining rights for U.M.W.A. Mr. Taylor's opposition to this idea was insuperable and adamant—but not negative. On the subject of whether or not labor should be given the power to bargain, the Chairman was of an open mind, and the net result of the conversations was a compromise, prototype of the formula we have already set forth. By that compromise Mr. Lewis's wage and hour demands were granted. But the U.M.W.A. was recognized as a bargaining agent *for its own members only* and the open shop preserved.

That is one supporting fact; the second was more spectacular. Some time after Mr. Taylor returned from Europe in the late fall, when the storm was gathering over Alfred P. Sloan, Jr., in the automobile country, a movement got under way among a number of the big industrialists for the formation of a "united front." Chief instigators of this idea were certain of the steel independents and General Motors, though (as Mr. Lewis has publicly stated) glass and "to a lesser extent coal" were on the fringes of it. Mr. Taylor went so far as to attend a meeting of the united front at which he was told that the time had come for a showdown against labor and that the allied industries must be prepared to dump their capital into a do-or-die fight. At which point Mr. Taylor arose and said that he would have nothing to do with the idea. He even went so far as to say that any such concerted action would be interpreted only as a capitalistic conspiracy to gang up on labor. So strong was his attitude that the united front fell apart.

Such, then, was the Chairman's faith in the Myron Taylor formula for industrial peace, which he had worked out that summer. And having come so far one might have expected him to plunge on. Characteristically, however, he did nothing of the kind. On one occasion, when discussing labor with business associates, he went so far as to wonder out loud whether it would be advisable to talk with Mr. Lewis; and one of the men present said, "Why of course you should. You did it in 1933 and you ought to try again." But even after this prodding Mr. Taylor hung back, not from indecision (for he is not the indecisive sort) but because, being instinctively a diplomat, he felt that the strategical moment had not yet arrived.

THE MOMENT

Thus the accidental meeting in the Mayflower, like all historical accidents, had been amply prepared, and as Mr. Taylor and Mr. Lewis stood chatting before the excited guests they knew of things more exciting than any of the guests could suspect. The next day we find Mr. Lewis in a Mayflower elevator on his way up to Mr. Taylor's suite. And a few minutes later the historic conferences had begun.

Here we may indulge in some speculation of a fairly foolproof variety. Neither Mr. Lewis nor Mr. Taylor will reveal what was discussed at that first meeting, but it seems clear that the sitdown strike at General Motors must have had some attention, and that Mr. Taylor must have expounded the principles of his formula—collective bargaining combined with the open shop. In this event he would have pointed out that if Mr. Lewis wanted to settle with General Motors, the closed shop and the checkoff would have to be thrown out of the window. Mr. Lewis has an intuitive and an agile mind. Whatever Mr. Taylor may have said or left unsaid, it seems certain that labor's chieftain left the conference with no illusions on most points. At any rate, his settlement with General Motors followed the formula closely.

Mr. Lewis and Mr. Taylor met again. And again. But such was the big laborite's skill in lumbering in and out of the crowded Mayflower that no one had the least suspicion of what he was up to, a few of the more observant Washington correspondents noting merely that he disappeared on several occasions without leaving any trace of himself. On January 14 Mr. Taylor swung out to Pittsburgh to plead for industrial peace at the opening of the new $10,000,000 plate mill at Homestead. But by the seventeenth he was back in Washington again. Here he found Mr. Lewis in one of his wildcat fighting moods, roaring at Alfred Sloan and calling upon the President to pay up for the support that labor had given him in the elections. The atmosphere of Mr. Taylor's suite after one of those hell-raising days, with the Chairman sitting thoughtfully in an armchair and Mr. Lewis trudging the floor, is better imagined than written. One must in any case admire the open-mindedness of the steel master no less than the huge courage of the laborite, who had the President of the United States and the automobile and steel industries on his hands at one and the same time. On the twenty-eighth, when Mr. Taylor left Washington, the friendly conspiracy was postponed. And on February 2 Mr. Lewis moved in person on Detroit.

*Mr Lewis
& Mr Taylor*

THE CRITICAL DAYS

What Mr. Lewis accomplished in Detroit has a direct bearing on our tale, but in order to simplify it we must transfer ourselves first to New York. There, on February 4, the coal operators met with Philip Murray, Mr. Lewis's smart Scotch lieutenant, to negotiate new contracts with the United Mine Workers. Embroiled with Mr. Sloan in Detroit and then laid up for a spell with flu, Mr. Lewis was unable to attend these meetings until February 17, when he settled himself into the St. Regis Hotel and went to work for his own U.M.W.A. But he did not spend all of his time at the coal conferences. Muffling his unforgettable physiognomy in his coat collar as best he could, he often slipped away and out of sight. And no one knows where. But it is a safe bet that if some curious idler had been standing in East Seventieth Street hard by Myron C. Taylor's triple house he would have seen a cab draw up night after night and a big man step out with his hat cocked stubbornly forward over his forehead.

The fact that Mr. Lewis came secretly and frequently to the house of steel is one of the reasons why the story of these negotiations has never been told. It was, to say the least, an embarrassing spot in which to argue the proletarian cause. But that aspect of the situation is only superficial. Mr. Taylor and Mr. Lewis had now come a long way toward understanding each other, and it did not much matter in whose house they conferred—the truth could be spoken just the same.

Indeed it is evident that back in Washington they had mistrusted each other: the big, voluble ex-miner on the one hand, who had knocked his way through the world; . . . and on the other, a patrician, a man who would have made his mark by the agility of his mental equipment, even if he had not had the most potent industrialists and financiers for his friends. Against Mr. Lewis's subtle and often playful imagination there was balanced Mr. Taylor's formal and often forbidding austerity. Against the hobbyless Sunday afternoons, when, as paterfamilias, Mr. Lewis thunders at any intruder who dares to come to him on business, there was weighed a warm interest in medieval tapestries and a modest private collection of Italian primitives. These were the minutiae that had to be attended to before history could be made—the amenities, moralities, and aesthetics difficult for reticent men to yield up, yet indispensable to the long process of bringing Mohammed and the mountain together. And these were the very things that came to light most easily in Mr. Taylor's house, where the tapestries and the primitives were hung.

The lucky thing was that Mr. Taylor, for all his formality, is a sociable sort of man who likes a foursome in the afternoon and a long, sparkling dinner table in the evening; and Mr. Lewis, while he is generally half aloof from the industrial tycoons, is a conversationalist of power and versatility who delights in nothing better than to exercise his wit among folk who have thought of labor leaders in terms of William Green. It was this interplay of conversation that led them on. Yet it is not to be supposed either that they spent their stolen evenings in defining the amenities. Now and then one of them would, so to speak, pull out the diapason, and the great, solid theme of steel would be heard, and rise up to engulf them both for an hour or so.

And it was during these tonic moments that Mr. Taylor, diplomatist extraordinary, executed his plot. It was a simple plot and certainly not reprehensible, but plot it was nevertheless. It consisted in erecting before Mr. Lewis, in vivid word pictures, the great, forbidding specter of U.S. Steel's Board of Directors. As a matter of fact Mr. Taylor had been consulting his Board ever since his return from Europe in September and had turned the heat on all the way while Mr. Lewis was in Detroit. And although he had met with considerable resistance to his new labor philosophy from half a dozen of the Directors, he had met with encouragement from as many others. Nevertheless Mr. Taylor did not dwell upon the encouragement. To Mr. Lewis rather he relayed the vigorous objections of men who had hundreds of thousands of employees on their aggregate payroll, and who reasoned that if C.I.O. were allowed to get a foothold in steel it would eventually invade every industry in the land. This opposition, never in reality an insuperable threat to his statesmanlike plan, became in Mr. Taylor's skillful hands a jack by which to lift labor into a trading mood. With the result that in the end Mr. Lewis traded out the closed shop just as Mr. Taylor had advised him to do (and as he did do) in the automobile strike.

It is probable, however, that Mr. Taylor had his Board already in hand by the time Mr. Lewis arrived at the St. Regis to attend to coal meetings. The arguments he used to convince them would lead us astray into complexities, but they may be summarized briefly as follows:

1. The steel industry was participating in the domestic prosperity and might even be on the verge of a boom. To become tied up in a labor war would be to forfeit net profits the like of which had not been seen since before the depression.

2. Besides the domestic boom, Britain was about to call for bids on steel for her new $7,000,000,000 armament program.

3. The Walsh-Healey Act had tied the industry up in knots that could be untied only by raising wages and shortening hours; but if these steps were taken ex C.I.O., Scotch Mr. Murray would claim them as victories for C.I.O. anyway.

4. One of the big jobs that Mr. Taylor had set himself when he took over the chairmanship was the reorganization of steel production. Without entering the intricacies of this subject, it is clear that a reorganization of production implied a considerable simplification in the labor structure. The Carnegie-Illinois Steel Co. (to cite one example only) had built up a fantastic system of wage scales resulting in no less than 11,000 different rates of pay applicable to 100,000 employees in twenty-eight mills. A wage structure as complicated as that is an almost insuperable obstacle to labor organizers, since it facilitates favoritism and job politics. But the system had backfired upon its inventors because it made a scientific analysis of production all but impossible. It was evident to anyone who thought about the situation objectively that a reliable contract with a vertical, industrial union such as that being organized by the S.W.O.C. would constitute a necessary first step toward a new and simplified industrial technique.

5. The C.I.O. drive in the steel country was probably the most intelligently directed labor drive ever organized in the United States, complete with a fast-footed legal staff, high political connections, and a counter espionage system that was feeding the La Follette Committee with information just as distasteful to the gentlemen on the Board of U.S. Steel as it was to their Chairman. And here Mr. Lewis's exploit at Detroit weighed heavily upon the minds entrusted with the destiny of big steel. Whether General Motors had had a right to eject the sitdowners from its plants did not seem to the gentlemen to be the question, because very obviously they could not have been ejected without bloodshed. But if this sort of thing could tie up the automobile industry, which had been hastily organized, what would prevent it from tying up steel, where the C.I.O. was firmly and forethoughtedly entrenched?

Moreover, it had begun to look very doubtful whether the steel operators could win a strike, at any rate in Pennsylvania. Time was when they could have called upon the trusty Coal and Iron Police, but that faithful little band of desperadoes had been outlawed some years previously by Governor Pinchot. And time was when they could have counted on Harrisburg for the state troops, but as of February, 1937, it looked as if the resources of Harrisburg would be thrown chiefly to the other side. The rise of Governor Murphy of Michigan into the national limelight had indeed been a disturbing phenomenon to Pennsylvania's Governor Earle, who had presidential ambitions and would like nothing better than a chance to eclipse Governor Murphy in the headlines by refusing the economic royalists the use of the state militia. Obviously any resistance from the operators would simply make good political fodder for Mr. Earle. Which was one expedient reason for not starting trouble.[2]

Obviously all these points could be summed up in the simple statement that the Corporation had an enormous dollars-and-cents stake in heading off an industrial war. But before the august Directors achieved unanimity on the matter, another war broke out on a different front.

THE INDEPENDENTS

Go back momentarily to June 29, 1936, when the Iron and Steel Institute issued its manifesto to labor. That document defined the attitude of the independents toward John L. Lewis and all other outsiders. But while the independents were holding this fixed position, Mr. Taylor had written his formula and taken steps to put it into action; and sooner or later a clash was inevitable. About the second week in February three of the independents, through the watchfulness with which all good industrialists compliment each other, got wind of the fact that Mr. Taylor and Mr. Lewis were holding conversations, and they went to see the Chairman. But before they got around to the subject, Mr. Taylor himself broached it. Inviting them to lunch with him in his office, he said that he was holding conversations with Mr. Lewis and he showed them the formula with which he was negotiating.

There ensued a heated debate, from which there emerged the fact that the independents wanted to meet the situation by raising wages. Mr. Taylor, however, did not want to raise wages. And for this he had two reasons. First, he believed that if Mr. Lewis were granted collective bargaining along the lines of the formula, the C.I.O. would not insist on a wage increase. Second, he said that he did not think that the wage increase was the point at issue out in the field. To the independents' insistence that it was, he replied that he was so differently informed that he wanted to check back with his own people. And with this the meeting was adjourned until a week later.

The next meeting came on Friday, February 26, and it broke the steel industry wide open. Mr. Taylor said that he had talked with his executives, who concurred with him that the wage issue was not the leading issue among the men. The independents, however, adhering to the policy by which the steel industry (but especially, be it noted, the Corporation) had lost ground to labor all summer, insisted that labor could best be handled by increasing wages, at the same time bolstering the company unions. Parenthetically it should be pointed out here that

[2] At the conclusion of the agreement Governor Earle wired warm congratulations to C.I.O. and Carnegie-Illinois.

the company-union idea had had a boomerang action in many mills, serving to educate the workers in organization practices; and in certain cases the C.I.O. had been able to swing these organizations into the ranks *in toto.* Whether because Mr. Taylor had this fact in mind, or because he was only part way through his negotiations with Mr. Lewis and believed that wages could be traded out, he refused to countenance an increase at that time, and he went so far as to say that he did not think he could sell the idea to his Board. So this meeting adjourned also, with the understanding that Mr. Taylor would consult the Board on Monday and reconfer on Tuesday.

Thereafter the pace became breathless. The Chairman had a long conversation with Mr. Lewis Friday night at which two other men were present who had been in and out of the situation all along. These were Thomas Moses, President of the H. C. Frick Coke Co., who handled details for Mr. Taylor, and Philip Murray, Mr. Lewis's smart, agressive lieutenant, who had been studying the steel situation since he was put in charge of the S.W.O.C. drive last spring. The next day (Saturday, February 27) Mr. Benjamin Fairless, President of the Carnegie-Illinois Steel Co., returning from a week's tour of his plants during which he had made a great number of speeches assuring the company unions that the management stood behind them, found a telegram on his desk. It was a brisk message requesting him to come to New York for an urgent conference on Sunday. Mr. Fairless went. Arriving in New York he stepped unawares into the situation that we have now traced from its origins. And having assimilated it as well as he could, he returned to Pittsburgh.

On Sunday night Mr. Taylor had a final meeting with Mr. Lewis. On Monday morning he met with his Board. And then things began to happen out in the steel country. About two o'clock independent spies arrived breathlessly in the offices of their executives to report that Mr. Benjamin Fairless and Mr. Philip Murray were about to sit down at a conference table at Carnegie-Illinois. Most of the executives did not credit the news, but at three o'clock Mr. William A. Irvin, President of U.S. Steel, called them all up in person and said that the C.I.O. and the Corporation were going to sit down that afternoon. Bending forward incredulously in his chair, one of the independents shouted, "I can't believe you. What time this afternoon?" Mr. Irvin said three o'clock. At this the steel master banged his fist on the desk. "It's three o'clock now!" he roared. And Mr. Irvin said, "So it is."

Thereafter the independents clutched their phones and began to crisscross the country with long-distance calls. The first news that the men in Mr. Fairless's office were S.W.O.C. representatives went on the wire at three twenty-six; and at three thirty-five Mr. Fairless handed out a statement verifying this fact. All during the conference the independents continued to check with each other. And they did so to such good effect that within an hour and forty-five minutes after the meeting ended no less than five of them had announced a new minimum wage, the first flash coming from Ernest Weir's National Steel Co. at 4:49 P.M.

Viewed in the calm light of history, this is the kind of affair in which it is impossible for the outsider to take sides. Mr. Taylor, it is now evident, was in an extremely delicate position. Though he had won Mr. Lewis's confidence and had obtained the backing of his Board, there was obviously no hope of swinging the independents over to his way of thinking; and in order to protect Mr. Lewis as well as himself, about the only thing to do was to beat them to the draw. If he had not done so his whole edifice might have collapsed, in which event this story would not have been written and the industrial world would not have been treated to the spectacle of the U.S. Steel Corp. and the C.I.O. shaking hands. Many men do not believe that they should have shaken hands. Many, many more believe that the handshake began a new era in industrial labor relations. At which point we can perhaps do no better than to quote the generous Mr. Lewis. He said:

> This agreement has been made possible by the farseeing vision and industrial statesmanship of Myron C. Taylor. From time to time over a period of several months in New York and Washington, Mr. Taylor and I have engaged in conversations and negotiations. We were each conscious of the great weight of responsibility and the far-reaching consequences attached to our decisions. Labor, industry, and the nation will be the beneficiaries.

In the form in which our story has been constructed, Mr. Taylor has been cast in the heroic role. But that is largely because Mr. Taylor's motives, being less obvious than those of Mr. Lewis, have been followed in closer detail. According to the laws of drama Mr. Lewis is the real hero because Mr. Lewis is in the midst of a great, unfinished struggle in which this episode represents only one advance. Both Mr. Taylor and Mr. Lewis tasted victory; but for Mr. Lewis that victory must sooner or later resolve itself again into strife, whereas for Mr. Taylor it is a monument, fixed and immovable. Mr. Taylor took the chair of the U.S. Steel Corp. with the expressed intention of resigning in the not too distant future, and so far as his career is concerned, he could tender that resignation tomorrow and the world would acclaim him a successful man. He is free at any time to follow his bent toward diplomacy, and the gossip that he will be the next Ambassador to the Court of St. James is worth paying some attention to, if only for that reason. No such fateful reward awaits Mr. Lewis, and one might add that none such is desired. The man who brought big steel to terms will probably die with his boots on.

"Little Steel" (1937) *

The strike in the twenty-seven plants of Republic, Youngstown Sheet & Tube, and Inland Steel broke . . . less than three months after U.S. Steel signed its agreement with the Steel Workers' Organizing Committee of the C.I.O., six weeks after the Supreme Court declared the Wagner Act constitutional, and five days after the union won a consent election, conducted by the NLRB, at the two great plants of Jones & Laughlin. . . . Before the outbreak of the strike in Little Steel, the S.W.O.C. could boast that it had negotiated 140 agreements, established 52 administrative offices, and brought 400,000 workers into 797 lodges.

All of which had brought an answer from the masters of Little Steel. Their argument against unions in general and the S.W.O.C. in particular distilled from opinions in steel journals, the speeches and writings of steel men, would run about like this: if the proportion of union members to total nonagricultural workers in the United States has remained below that of the European democracies, it has not been because collective bargaining has been resisted more strenuously by American employers. It has been because American workmen are not greatly interested in national labor unions. From this it follows that national unions are foreign importations, the outgrowth of the rigid class divisions of Europe. From this point of view the issue of collective bargaining is false, since these people maintain that local unions, independent unions, employee-representation plans, and the like provide collective bargaining. Where the Labor Board has decided in a number of cases that such organizations are simply the old-fashioned company unions, revamped to comply with the Wagner Act, the answer is that the Labor Board is prejudiced and unfair. The figures on the increase of union membership are answered by the assertion that the figures are exaggerated, that most members do not pay their dues, and that the labor advance we have described is less a mass movement than the result of a political alliance between the Administration and the leaders of organized labor—who, even if their claims are granted, represent only a small percentage of the total industrial population. This point of view, to be sure, is found in other circles than in steel, but in no other industry has it been so vehemently advanced. "I won't have a contract, verbal or written," said Mr. Girdler, "with an

* From "Little Steel," *Fortune*, XVI (November, 1937), 166, 168, 171-172, 174, 176. Copyright 1937 by Time Inc. Reprinted by special permission.

irresponsible, racketeering, violent, communistic body like the C.I.O., and until they pass a law making me do it, I am not going to do it." . . .

From the bridges over the Mahoning at Youngstown you can look down upon the giant byproduct coke ovens, the blast furnaces, the open-hearth furnaces, the Bessemer converters, the blooming mills, the billet and bar mills, the skelp mills, and the spike plant of Republic's Youngstown works; on the smaller mills of Youngstown Sheet & Tube, set almost in the center of the city. You can look down, too, upon a stretch of grim and smoke-darkened streets, on the section given over to its lurid night life, beside the fence surrounding the Youngstown Sheet & Tube Works. You can see the Bessemer converter that stands like a howitzer beside the red-light district, and from which flames periodically shoot skyward with a volcanic roar, blanching the street with a sulphurous light. You can look down upon a section of gray wooden houses where live a good share of Youngstown's 32,938 foreign-born, alongside her 14,552 Negroes. And on the far side you can see the tree-shaded residential streets, equally remote from the mills and the slums, so closely knit that dwellers there insist that Youngstown, for all its 170,000, is essentially a small town.

Up and down the Mahoning, as the strike got under way, the picket lines formed. They were established at mill gates and along the railroad embankments, organized into groups of five doing six-hour turns, with one leader for each group, four division captains (one for each turn), and a head picket. Forty-two cars patrolled the Campbell picket line. In Warren the line stretched over the eight-mile circuit around the Republic plant. In Monroe it crossed the road beside the Raisin River that led to the main gate. In South Chicago, on the first day of the strike, it formed near the plant entrance at 116th Street and Burley Avenue, but was dispersed by the police, and twenty-three pickets were arrested. Within Republic's plants, by the company's count, a large number of men were still at work—2,400 in Warren, 1,400 in South Chicago, "several hundred" at Niles, 2,900 at Buffalo—and food was brought in to them by airplane and sent parcel post. At Youngstown a train, crashing through the picket line at Youngstown Steel & Tube, led to violence in the first days of the strike. The planes were fired on, the mails were stopped, and after the train at Youngstown crashed through the picket line pickets cut the rails with acetylene torches.

In every strike the men who remain at work—the loyal workers of embattled management, the scabs of strikers—draw on themselves the accumulated resentment of the picket lines. But in the strike in Little

Steel, for reasons that will presently become apparent, the status of non-striking employees decidedly changed, and with it there was an equally momentous change in the attitude of the union toward them. It was to protect these loyal workers, Republic Steel claimed, that it armed its plants. (92 riot guns, 2,295 long-range projectiles—tear and sickening gas —326 short-range gas cartridges, and 2,029 gas grenades were purchased by Republic and its subsidiaries in May and June—a total expenditure of $43,901.) And the police of Chicago claimed that it was while protecting the 1,400 (company's figure) workers who remained in the South Chicago works of Republic Steel, on Memorial Day, when the strike was four days old, that the pickets were dispersed, with four killed outright, six fatally injured, and ninety wounded, some thirty of them by gunfire.

Read the report of the La Follette Committee on what it calls the Memorial Day incident and you will find a story as savage as any in the dark annals of American labor struggles. You will read of the strike starting on the day of the general strike call, of gas costing $3,300 stored in the plant, of how the first picket line was dispersed, with twenty-three arrested, and how, afterward, Mayor Kelly stated that peaceful picketing would be permitted. You will read of the increased police force around the plant, of a mass meeting called near the factory, followed by a march toward it to establish the picket lines over "a stretch of flat, waste, sparsely inhabited prairie land east of and adjacent to the South Chicago plant of the steel corporation—the plant itself is bounded on the west by the Calumet River, on the north by steel scrap piles, the south by low prairie land, and on the east by a barbed-wire-topped fence and the tracks of the Pennsylvania Railroad." You will read also of the marchers approaching the line of 264 police, of a discussion about picketing suddenly interrupted by a stick thrown by the inevitable unknown, a tear gas bomb tossed at the moment the cameraman was changing his lenses, and, after a graphic report of the subsequent gunfire, the brutal treatment of the injured, and the sixty-seven arrests, the grim conclusion that "the consequences of the Memorial Day encounter were clearly avoidable by the police." [1]

As has been pointed out in the Remington Rand strike, the back-to-work movement of contemporary strikes occupies the center of the stage. Early in the Little Steel strike Philip Murray charged that the Mohawk Valley Formula was being followed step by step, and when the strike spread to Johnstown *The New York Times* correspondent, F. Raymond Daniell, found its pattern repeated in the events that led to the formation

[1] The verdict of the coroner's jury was made public the day before the report of the La Follette Committee. The shootings were termed "justifiable homicide."

of a Citizens' Committee and a demand for the reopening of Bethlehem's Cambria plant. But a strike involving 83,000 and extending over seven states is a vastly different affair from one in a small city dependent upon a single industry, and only at Monroe, Michigan (where the small Republic-owned Newton Steel Co.'s plant was an unimportant unit in Republic's production, but of vital consequence to the community), did events correspond to those in Ilion.

There the mayor polled the employees to determine how many wanted to return to work. Out of a total of 1,350, it was officially claimed 826 voted for, 20 against, and 504 did not vote. After some 300 men had been deputized, a date was set for opening the plant. It was postponed at Governor Murphy's request. He called a conference in Lansing, to be attended by the mayor, the union organizer, and representatives of the back-to-work movement. While the conference was on, at three in the afternoon of June 10, some 200 deputies marched to the picket line, ahead of the members of the back-to-work movement, organized into an independent union. Given two minutes to open the road, the picket captain gained twenty minutes more in order to telephone Governor Murphy. But while negotiations were going on the ubiquitous tear gas bomb was thrown toward the pickets while a stone simultaneously sailed toward the deputies, and within ten minutes the pickets were in flight, at least nine automobiles were dumped into the Raisin River by the deputies, and the nonstriking employees returned to work.

At Massillon the back-to-work movement ran into greater difficulties and led to a more tragic ending. There the chief of Massillon's police force of eighteen men refused to permit a poll to be taken because, he said, it would cause trouble unless conducted by the Labor Board. But after a month in which, he testified, he was warned by Republic officials that if the mills closed Massillon would be "just a junction with no need for a mayor or a chief of police," and during which he was urged to deputize special policemen and guards, he blew up: "I said all right I would appoint the whole damn outfit. I would give them everything they wanted." The deputies were sworn in and armed. In spite of the unwillingness of the officials to take this course on the grounds that violence would follow, nothing happened until the night of Sunday, July 11, when Police Chief Switter took "a little drive in the country for a glass of beer." When he returned he found that in his absence a riot in front of union headquarters had cost the life of a union member, that thirteen had been injured, and 160 arrested.

But for observing the process by which a full-grown back-to-work movement comes into being (as well as the tension it may create), Youngstown provides a better specimen for study than smaller communities. In the first days of the strike the Independent Association of Republic Employees and the Independent Society of Workers of Youngstown Sheet & Tube opened adjoining offices in the Dollar Savings & Trust Co. ("paying no rent," said the Labor Board's investigator sourly) and began collecting signatures of employees who wanted to return to work. While Governor Davey was calling peace conferences, airplanes were dropping food into the plants and the back-to-work movement spread among the pleasant homes of Norwood Avenue and Poland Manor—an intense drive made up of employees who did not support the strike, of businessmen who believed that a minority of pickets was preventing the majority of employees from working, of clubwomen who telephoned their resolutions to Boake Carter, wrote letters to the President, and sent a delegation to Governor Davey at three in the morning.

The strike was in its third week when Secretary of Labor Perkins appointed a Steel Mediation Board. President Roosevelt declared that companies willing to make oral agreements should put them into writing, and another night riot left two dead and some thirty to fifty injured in Youngstown. The Steel Mediation Board negotiations soon broke down, not over the question of a signed agreement, but over a proposal that the companies recognize the S.W.O.C. pending Labor Board election, the agreements to be torn up in plants where the union lost. The Senate Post Office inquiry was proceeding. That inquiry resembled a La Follette Committee hearing turned around, for in place of reports of violence against strikers by police or company guards, it was filled with reports of violence by pickets against nonstriking workers—stories of men beaten, stripped, or driven from home. In Youngstown the sheriff deputized a hundred men, and Republic Steel and Youngstown Sheet & Tube had already announced that their plants would be reopened on Tuesday morning, June 22. "In the name of God and the overwhelming majority of steel workers of Youngstown," the union wired the President, ". . . we urge you to immediately intervene in this critical hour and avoid a calamity and disaster that Ohio may remember for decades to come." The United Labor Congress threatened a general strike, the truck drivers struck, union sympathizers streamed into town. Word came at midnight that the mediation conference had broken down, and in the office building of Youngstown Sheet & Tube reporters crowded into two rooms overlooking Shop 14, where the heaviest concentration of pickets was massed before the gates. After midnight word came that by the President's request the mills would not reopen. At Governor Davey's order 5,000 National Guardsmen marched in, and in the morning to the accompaniment of cheers from the picket lines, the tension was broken. And, although it was not apparent until later, so was the strike.

Three days later on June 25 Governor Davey completely reversed his position and, issuing a statement, "the right to work is sacred," ordered National Guardsmen to protect returning workers. The picket lines had been withdrawn, and the Guard now made the reestablishment of the picket line impossible. Attempts to bring in supplementary pickets from Akron and elsewhere were thwarted and simultaneously arrests of strikers and sympathizers began—225 were arrested in Youngstown alone.

In terms of its immediate importance, the Little Steel strike is consequently involved with politics—with the union's belief that it had Governor Davey's support no less than with the labor policy of the Administration, and with whatever decisions were forming in Franklin D. Roosevelt's mind when he wished a plague on the house of John L. Lewis and on the house of Tom Girdler. . . .

At present the C.I.O.'s partisans insist that, although the union lost the strike, the companies did not win. If the employers believe that the strike turned public opinion against the C.I.O., the union believes just as strongly that public opinion was turned against the companies because of Girdler's refusal to settle. . . . Union officials are also careful to point out that the loss of the strike in Little Steel bears no relation to the loss of the steel strike of 1919, which stopped organizing efforts in steel for twelve years.

They further point out that the Labor Board hearings in the steel companies are still proceeding. Eventually, they expect, elections will be ordered in the plants. Which leads to the profound change in contemporary strikes that the steel strike demonstrated. When it became apparent that the strike could not succeed, the union's attitude toward the men remaining at work underwent a transformation. The nonstriking workers, the historic object of resentment in labor disputes, became the voters of the future, to be appealed to as potential supporters rather than denounced as scabs. This development occurred too late in the steel strike to be of great importance. What it means for the future conduct of unions depends on the next stage in the evolution of the National Labor Relations Board.

National Labor Relations Board (1938) *

ORDER

Upon the basis of the above findings of fact and conclusions of law, and pursuant to Section 10 (c) of the National Labor Relations Act, the National Labor Relations Board hereby orders that the respondent, Re-

* From "In the Matter of Republic Steel Corporation and Steel Workers Organizing Committee," Case No. C-184, decided October 18, 1938. *Decisions and Orders of the National Labor Relations Board*, IX, October 1, 1938-November 30, 1938 (Washington: U.S. Government Printing Office, 1939), 400-404.

public Steel Corporation, and its officers, agents, successors, and assigns, shall:

1. Cease and desist from:

(a) Dominating or interfering with the formation of any labor organization of its employees or contributing financial or other support thereto;

(b) Discouraging membership in the Amalgamated Association of Iron, Steel, and Tin Workers of North America or the Steel Workers Organizing Committee or any other labor organization of its employees, by discharging and refusing to reinstate employees, or otherwise discriminating in regard to hire or tenure of employment or any term or condition of employment or by threats of such discrimination;

(c) In any other manner interfering with, restraining, or coercing its employees in the exercise of their right to self-organization, to form, join, or assist labor organizations, to bargain collectively through representatives of their choosing, and to engage in concerted activities for the purpose of collective bargaining or other mutual aid and protection as guaranteed in Section 7 of the Act.

2. Take the following affirmative action which the Board finds will effectuate the policies of the Act.

(a) Withdraw all recognition from the Plan of Employee Representation, and its successors. . . .

[(b)-(g) orders reinstatement and back pay to "employees laid off, discharged, and refused reinstatement prior to or during the strike; strikers, upon application."]

(h) Post immediately in conspicuous places in its plants, . . . and maintain for a period of at least sixty (60) consecutive days, notices to its employees stating that the respondent will cease and desist in the manner aforesaid. . . .

VI. Labor at Mid-Century:
Memories and Realities

On the eve of World War II, the combined efforts of the A.F. of L. and the C.I.O. had substantially reduced the number of unorganized American workers. But admittedly much work remained to be done, especially in the South where the steady movement of northern industry and the existence of a cheap labor pool created new organizational challenges. Although unions won additional economic gains for their members in the postwar years, they made little progress against the unorganized; instead, union leaders had to devote an increasing amount of time to the complex machinery of collective bargaining, the threat of legislative restrictions, growing unemployment, and the gnawing problem of internal corruption. In the era of the cold war and the search for internal security, the two major labor federations sought to hammer home their essential conservatism.

The position of organized labor in postwar American society has occasioned considerable debate. The labor movement, some have argued, has fallen a victim to bureaucratization, gross materialism, petty racketeering, and respectability; age and prosperity have made it too self-satisfied and apathetic; liberals and intellectuals no longer look to it as a liberalizing influence and the general public has lost much of its previous "underdog" sympathy. These factors, the critics conclude, have deprived organized labor of a militant faith which had once enabled it to organize the unorganized. "To sum up," one such critic wrote, "the labor movement is not a leader in the nation today. It does not evoke an image of the underdog, the champion of progress, the advocate of the brotherhood of man. It is, in the mind of the general public, another 'special interest.' "

Some union leaders will concede the validity of much if not all of this criticism, for they, too, are deeply concerned with the present drift of organized labor. Although it is still deemed essential to keep wages apace with the rising cost of living and win additional "fringe" benefits for the membership, some admit that this is not enough, that organized labor must deal more forcefully with the problem of the unorganized, the corrupt, and the apathetic, and prepare to face the even more formidable challenge of automation and technological unemployment. Problems such as these pose crucial tests for the professional trade unionists—the organization men of labor. And the vitality of the labor movement as a force in American society may well depend on the outcome.

"The Haunted Hall: I.W.W. at Fifty"—Dan Wakefield (1955) *

You don't remember the Wobblies. You were too young. Or else not even born yet. There has never been anything like them, before or since. They called themselves materialist-economists but what they really were was a religion. They were workstiffs and bindlebums like you and me, but they were welded together by a vision we don't possess.

From Here to Eternity by James Jones

Bob Willock is a man in an empty room whose windows provide slanting glimpses of Wall Street towers, to the east, and the waterfront, to the west. It is the meeting hall of the Manhattan branch of the Industrial Workers of the World—"the Wobblies"—an organization sustained by a vision that refuses to die in the face of all facts and funeral rites. The IWW is fifty years old now and largely forgotten, but the vision that made it the greatest radical movement in American labor still holds men like Bob Willock, who stared at it once, to the several scattered halls across the country that are so full of memories and empty of men.

The memories are many—riding the rails to Spokane to support fellow workers in the free speech fights of the west, following the harvest with the dreams of better wages and the songs of Joe Hill, striking and picketing the textile mills at Lawrence, Massachusetts, when Joe Ettor raised his voice above the jailings and killings to tell the employers that "you can't weave cloth with bayonets."

The men are few—but the miracle is that there are any left at all. What sort of men in our practical times have the heart to stay loyal to a vision the world all around them laughs off as obsolete?

Bob Willock went to sea out of Galveston in 1925 on the old Savannah line (like most of the stuff of his past, it is gone now) and by the time he docked in Boston a fellow on board had persuaded him to take out a Wobbly book. He didn't think much about it at the time but two years later he was trying to ship from the gulf again and a fellow from the International Seamen's Union tried to shake him down for extra dough to get an ISU book. Bob wouldn't pay and went around to the Wobbly hall. They got him a ship on condition he'd strike with the other Wobbly crewmen against the line's plan for cutting the deckhands and

---

* Dan Wakefield, "The Haunted Hall: I.W.W. at Fifty," *Dissent*, III (1956), 414-419. Reprinted by permission of *Dissent*.

lengthening the watch, and he did, and the ship sailed with full crew and customary hours and Bob has been a Wobbly ever since. For the last six years he has alternated between the sea and the job of secretary of the IWW Marine Transport Workers Union, No. 510, Manhattan Branch.

It occupies a fading, lime-colored room above a Chinese laundry on Broad Street, and by the rules and traditions of the IWW, Bob Willock can't get paid more to run it than the average wage of the workers who belong. At the back of the hall a partition creates his home and office, which consists of a hotplate, a folding bed, a large cluttered desk, and a bookcase. The Wobblies still read—just as they did in the early days when IWW migratory workers took their books from harvest to harvest in the west—and they talk, and remember. That is almost all they have left, and that is primarily what Bob Willock's job is. He keeps a pot of coffee on and passes the time with the few who walk in from the past, like the "fellow who used to be a cellmate of Big Bill Haywood at Leavenworth, drops by just about every Sunday, just to talk."

"We really aren't doing any organizing now," Bob told a visitor not long ago. "The fellows who still belong, it's mostly an ideal with them. You can't keep paying dues on two unions, and the one that gets you a job is the one you take."

The cause lost most of its remaining missionaries in 1949 when the U.S. government administered the most recent of the many deathblows that the IWW has absorbed. It was placed on the Attorney-General's list of subversive organizations because its membership, estimated at 1,400 at the time, was feared as a group that "seeks to alter the form of government of the United States by unconstitutional means." W. H. Westman, the IWW General Secretary-Treasurer, wrote to Tom Clark to ask for a reversal of the ruling, or at least an explanation of it, but was granted neither, and the ailing Wobbly treasury was too weak to do battle with the government it threatened by carrying the matter into court.

Big Bill Haywood had tried to explain back in 1918 at the trial of the 101 Wobbly leaders indicted for subversive activities that the Wobbly dream was not political at all; that it didn't seek to change the form of economy; that its aim was to organize industrially to "form the structure of the new society within the shell of the old."

Those leaders were left to form the new society within the jails of the old, and when Warren Harding granted a commutation of sentence four years later, the leaders came out with their vision clouded, and the IWW was never quite the same. Haywood said to Ralph Chaplin once that "the hands of our people are calloused and scarred from trying to make a dream come true," and after four years at Cook County Jail and Leavenworth, the hearts were scarred, too. Haywood and George Andreytchine went to Russia, and the loss was the deepest the IWW had to bear.

The Wobblies had lost their leaders before, but this was a different kind of loss. It was one thing to lose Frank Little to a lynching mob when he tried to organize the miners in Butte, Montana; and to lose Joe Hill to a firing squad in Salt Lake City and be able to tell the world his last words were "Don't mourn for me—organize!" It was quite another thing to lose Haywood and Andreytchine to a foreign land.

There were others, later, who didn't go physically to Russia but moved spiritually to the Communist party, and the party's activities in the United States after the First World War were one of the vital drains on the health of the IWW. It was one of the deepest blows of all, in the way that Haywood's exile was, to see old Wobbly leaders exchange the grass-roots American radicalism of the IWW for the Soviet-grown dream of the party. In 1923 the IWW paper *Industrial Solidarity* called across the ideological miles to its former Fellow Worker William Z. Foster with a kind of brotherly message to a black sheep who'd strayed away from home for good:

> Willie, you may print a ton of *Labor Heralds* each month in the year, and fill them from cover to cover with robber, thief, highjack. You may shout reactionary, yellow, to the top of your breath, but after it is all over, the IWW will still be the IWW that it was when you were third cook in that lumber camp in the Northwest.

Elizabeth Gurley Flynn went, too, and Earl Browder, and many others. Those that remained were often bruised and bullied by the Communists who stole so much of their thunder and used it against them. Ralph Chaplin, the IWW poet and editor, was speaking for the Wobblies at a soapbox meeting in Chicago in the Thirties when a Communist youth group tried to lead his crowd away. They called him a reactionary and finally drowned out his voice by singing "Solidarity Forever"—the song he had written ten years before for the IWW.

Assignment to the subversive list was a particularly unpleasant irony for the Wobblies, who had fought the Communists right down the line, and were battered by them as they were battered by the employers, and the ranks of Respectability. The MTWU of the IWW had fought them on the waterfront throughout the Thirties when not many others were fighting them; and for their efforts the Wobblies now bear a "subversive" brand, and that is one more factor in their loneliness. Their old friends on the waterfront must now risk a taint by even coming to see them, and

Manhattan Branch 510 hasn't had enough men to hold a meeting in a year.

"It used to be we had to have fifteen men for a quorum," Bob Willock told his visitor. "This union's mostly transient, though, you know. We changed it to seven a few years back, but there hasn't been that many to hold a meeting with for, well, I guess about a year now."

The afternoon the visitor came to ask questions, there were only two men, besides Bob. "Not too many years ago," he said, "this hall was so crowded you couldn't get inside the door at this time of night.

The old fellows used to drop by for old times' sake, even though they didn't belong any more. But then, a few years back, the other unions moved their halls uptown, and it was too far to come."

There is a tall, straight lighthouse with bold initials "IWW" and two white beams shining out from its tower. Churning against it from every side are tidal waves pouring from a dark region labeled "Reaction" and written in the waves are the symbols "CIO," "AFL," "NLRB," a swastika, and a hammer-and-sickle.

The scene appears in a three-column, page one cartoon of *The Industrial Worker,* official fortnightly newspaper of the IWW. Unread copies, stacked in piles according to dates, clutter a table in the corner of the Manhattan Wobbly hall.

The visitor picked up an issue from the pile at the front, unfurled the four pages to their flag-like width, and noticed two large portraits. One was of Wesley Everest (killed by a mob in a raid on his union hall at Centralia, Wash., Nov. 11, 1919); the other was of Joe Hill (shot by a firing squad in Salt Lake City for a disputed murder case after organizing a strike nearby, Nov. 19, 1915). On the first page of the paper is a black-bordered list of eighteen IWW members killed while serving the union on various dates of past Novembers, and the heading is "In November We Remember." The most recent date is 1927.

The dates, the pictures, the old style seven-column makeup, the poetry, bear that unmistakable flavor of the past that is a part of all yellowing papers. But the pages are neither yellowing nor flaking—they are white, and the date of the issue is November 14, 1955.

It is typical of current issues of the paper, anchored so deeply in days gone by. The stories that aren't reprints from other publications usually reach toward the glories of the past, often with an uneasy sense that they might be lost in the vast indifference of the present. The lead story of the issue of September 19, 1955 is topped by a triple-deck head that reads "REMEMBER THE GREAT UNNAMED WHO LABORED IN OBSCURITY FOR HUMAN ADVANCEMENT."

The paper depends by tradition and financial necessity on contributions from fellow workers, reporting conditions "at the point of production." The reports now are few because the fellow workers are few, but there are still scattered words in the fiery traditions of the past, like the message beneath the bold "Organize Idaho" head on the front page of the October 31, 1955 issue. It is a summary straight from the point of production describing the state of disorganization among the Idaho lumbermen, and it is signed by "Idaho Jack."

But we know, unhappily, that no one today is named "Idaho Jack"— and we have to surmise that this faithful fellow worker is one who knew the west in the days when "Wobbly" was a dangerous and glorious word, and action by the IWW was bringing shorter hours, livable housing facilities, and enough clear bedding to eliminate the "bindle stiff" from the woods. The bindle stiff had to roll his blankets in a bundle and hoist it on his back from the long hard journeys from camp to camp, but even with dirty bedding his plight was more romantic, if more difficult, than that of the lumbermen Idaho Jack sees working today.

The new woodsmen drive their cars to the mountains and sleep overnight in the back seat, cooking their meals close by. It takes some of them four hours to drive to the woods but they don't want to batch it or camp any more, and the eyes of Idaho Jack must be sore for the sight of a bindle stiff.

Their counterparts of the waterfront are the men Bob Willock found when he went to sea the last time. "They're in debt with cars and television sets," he said. "They sat around after mess according to who had what kind of cars—the Fords in one corner, the Pontiacs over here, maybe a fellow with a Mercury talking to a fellow with a Dodge. All of 'em telling about what they get to the gallon."

To ask why the IWW is almost dead is perhaps to ask where the "old worker," the generic type "Wobbly" has gone—for his disappearance, more than all the deadly events that befell the organization, lies at the root of the IWW's obsolescence in 1955. While Walter Reuther negotiated for the Guaranteed Annual Wage with Ford in the Spring of '54, the auto workers hoped their leaders would let them off picket duty so they could get in some fishing and ball games. They stood outside the plant with their portable radios, listening to the latest rock-and-roll music; and the Wobblies who carried the picket signs in spite of bullets and tar and feathers at Lawrence and Paterson, McKees Rock and Butte, Bingham Canyon and Everett, became official ghosts of history.

Bob Willock wasn't able to get to the fiftieth anniversary convention of the IWW held last year in Chicago, and the Manhattan seamen's branch was represented by "a fellow who used to be here with us who's out in the west now." The fellow was one of sixteen delegates who met in the IWW national headquarters hall at 2422 Halstead Street.

The talk was mainly memories, some of them stretching back to 1905 when 203 delegates met for the first IWW convention, and listened to Big Bill Haywood open the proceedings. The Marxist sense of history was heavily upon him, and he told the assembled delegates that this was "The Continental Congress of the Working Class."

The words were proud and conceivably true, for when Haywood looked from the speaker's stand out across the faces of several hundred delegates he knew they represented more than 100,000 workers. His dream was big and that moment it was bright and untroubled by the blood-dimmed future of the organization that would find itself huddled in an almost empty room in Chicago fifty years later with sixteen delegates representing something like 600 men from nine branches across the country.

The Industrial Worker still pushes for recruitment, and many of its loyal readers try—though there seems to be only frustration for the effort, whether the prospective recruits be young men or old. C. D. Van Nostrand has tried the young, and he wrote from Des Moines that "I have talked to workers of the plant about lining up with the IWW but it was like talking to little boys who could not understand what I was talking about."

Bob Willock has tried the old, and he says it's like this:

I see 'em around the waterfront and they come up and slap me on the back and say "Hey, Bob, how's about having a drink? Listen Bob, how much do I owe on my dues? I been meaning to come up and pay back the dues I owe. How much do I owe now?"

I ask 'em how long it's been since they paid and they say "I dunno, Bob, it's been a good while. Don't you have the records up there at the hall?"

"Some," I say. And they say "Well, listen, Bob, I'll be up to settle with you, see? I'll be up real soon." And then they find somebody else to have a drink with and that's the end of it.

The world has moved up the street but Bob Willock stays fast to his drafty hall, like his fellow survivors in the outposts remaining. As long as they live, the IWW will live, and when they die, the IWW will die.

"What Really Ails the Unions" (1959) *

The leaders of organized labor have seldom sounded so isolated, or so remote from reality, as they sounded this past month. Their Labor Day messages and their oratory at the A.F.L.-C.I.O. convention sought to create the impression that the principal problems facing labor were manufactured in the Eighty-sixth Congress, where a "reactionary coalition" inspired by "big business leaders" had passed an "N.A.M. bill." Jim Carey of the Electrical Workers Union informed a television audience that the passage of the Landrum-Griffin bill was another step toward fascism. Our labor leaders sounded, in other words, pretty much as they had sounded in 1947, after the passage of Taft-Hartley; but this time the rhetoric had an archaic, almost quaint, ring to it, and nobody took it very seriously.

Organized labor has in fact been drifting away from the main currents of American life, and in several different ways it is growing weaker. For one thing, the unions have simply stopped growing: the labor force continues to expand, but its greatest expansion has been in areas (e.g., the South) and occupations (e.g., white-collar work) that have traditionally resisted unionism. Only a few labor leaders seem to be aware of this broad problem.

And no United States labor leaders have shown any awareness that, somewhere along the way these past ten years or so, organized labor has also lost a kind of moral strength it once possessed. Its pronouncements are no longer taken seriously even within the labor movement. With only a very few exceptions (e.g., John L. Lewis), the Gompers-era chieftains who built up the A.F. of L. are now gone from the scene, and replaced, in many instances, by rather ordinary bureaucrats who manifestly do not have much of anything on their minds. The men who built up the C.I.O. in the Thirties are still on the job, but beginning to look old and tired and incapable of providing much inspiration. Their successors tend to be timeservers, and to provide less inspiration.

The sad fact is that the United States labor movement no longer attracts the kind of energetic young idealists who once poured into it by the thousands. It can no longer plausibly claim that it is bent on reforming our society or even that it speaks for the underprivileged. And for all these reasons it has been largely deserted by the intellectuals and liberals who were once a pillar of union strength in the United States.

* "What Really Ails the Unions," an editorial from *Fortune* Magazine, LX (October, 1959), 107-108. Copyright 1959 by Time Inc. Reprinted by special permission.

Indeed, one of the most interesting aspects of the new labor legislation is the nonpartisan spirit in which it was adopted. Toward the end of the long congressional debates on this "tough" bill, it seemed as though the bill were scarcely controversial; legislators who voice the union line seem to be almost nonexistent these days. Senate liberals like Paul Douglas and Hubert Humphrey, who had shouted themselves hoarse against Taft-Hartley, this time stood on the sidelines, and finally voted for the bill without a murmur. Even Pat McNamara, who went to Congress after eighteen years as president of a Detroit pipefitters' local ended up among the ninety-five Senators who voted yea.

NO MORE CRUSADES

In part, of course, organized labor has been deserted by the liberals because of the McClellan Committee's revelations of union corruption and violence; three years of such testimony, much of it genuinely surprising even to the unions' enemies, obviously shook the loyalty of the unions' friends. But much more than corruption and violence are involved in the new isolation of the labor movement. Consider the reaction of the United States public to the 1959 steel strike, the longest in the industry's history.

The strike is widely regarded as a simple power struggle. Even the steel workers themselves seem to be under no illusion that they are participating in any kind of "crusade"; most of the reporters who have interviewed rank-and-file strikers found them stoically resigned to the hardships of the strike, hopeful that the union leadership knew what it was doing, and persuaded that the only big issue was whether they could wrestle a few more cents per hour out of the companies.

It is instructive to contrast these attitudes with those evoked by the 1949 steel strike. A decade ago, the steelworkers felt themselves to be "underdogs" in United States society, and their demand for pensions was regarded by liberals as a crusade to bring a greater measure of human dignity to plain workers.

What has happened to the steelworkers—and to unions as a whole— since 1949? The most important thing that has happened is ten years of prosperity. Since the 1949 strike, real hourly earnings in the steel industry have risen by fifty per cent. Annual earnings also rose sharply; and even in 1957 and 1958, when these earnings were affected by the recession layoffs, more than sixty per cent of the steel industry's production workers made over $4,800, and about thirty per cent of them made over $6,000.

Like members of other unions, the steelworkers are increasingly congregated in the "middle-income" groups, and are increasingly acting like "middle-class" citizens. *Fortune* has already noted, in its series on the Markets of the Sixties, the proliferation of "blue-collar suburbs"; of auto workers' wives shopping at Hudson's in Detroit, instead of at Sears, Roebuck; of machinists who take vacations in Florida (see "The New Masses," May, 1959). It's nice to have the machinists on the beach in Florida. But it's easy to understand why no one except the machinists really cares whether they get another 10 cents an hour.

THE TIDE IS RECEDING

What made those grandiose Labor Day speeches seem especially unreal was their attempt to portray the union movement as a rising tide; the Labor Day parade in New York, in which 100,000 unionists actually did march, was also designed to create an impression of massive strength. Yet the fact is that union members are a dwindling minority in the United States. Membership fell from a peak of 17,500,000 in 1956 to about 17 million in 1958. Of course, the recession had a lot to do with this decline, but in 1959 membership had not picked up nearly so fast as employment.

Much of this decline has been caused by automation and the new technology of United States industry. The machines have displaced large numbers of semiskilled workers and at the same time have tended to "professionalize" many skilled workers, who are beginning to look more like technicians and to think more like white-collar workers. In short, the blue-collar men who have traditionally been the main "market" for union organization are becoming harder to find. In 1947 they made up forty per cent of the labor force; today they amount to about thirty-seven per cent, and by 1970 the figure will be down to thirty-one per cent. (For more on these trends see "The Decade of the Discretionary Dollar," *Fortune*, June, 1959.) Meanwhile there has been a marked increase in white-collar workers—who are notoriously poor union material.

A few union leaders are doing something constructive about the dislocations caused by automation. At Armour & Co., for example, the two meat-packing unions have displayed rare common sense. Like other packers, Armour is trying to escape from its profit squeeze by closing obsolete plants, relocating its facilities, and installing automatic machinery to increase productivity. . . . This program obviously threatens the jobs of thousands of workers whose skills will no longer fit the technology of the meat industry.

The first inclination of the two unions at Armour was to demand that the company freeze employment and shorten the work week to spread the jobs around. But when the company proposed a plan to soften the impact of automation, the union wisely accepted it.

Under the new plan, Armour will contribute one cent for every hundredweight of meat shipped, up to a total of $500,000. The fund, to be administered by a committee of four management and four labor representatives, with a neutral chairman, will be used to train employees in the skills required by the new machines, and to assist displaced workers in moving to jobs in other parts of the country. Thus the unions at Armour have won a voice with management in dealing with the dislocations that result from technological change.

LABOR'S NEXT PHASE

The Armour experience suggests one of the good uses to which unionism can be put in the future. Originally, the principal mission of the unions was to prevent workers from being "pushed around" by their employers. The unions' next big mission may be to see that workers, including even those $5,000-a-year workers, don't get "pushed around" by the new technology.

But unfortunately for American labor not enough of its leaders appear to have the capacity to cope with this situation. Union leaders seem hardly aware that they are moving into a new and difficult phase of the movement's history, and that they can no longer count on the unquestioning sympathy and support of a large section of the public. For the first time in a quarter of a century, labor's spokesmen have to argue the unions' case before a predominantly skeptical audience. They aren't going to make much headway talking in a dead language.

"Organizing the Unorganized"—The Nation (1955) *

When John W. Livingston, director of organizing for the merging A.F. of L.-C.I.O., surveys his job, he will be looking beyond heavy industry, public utilities, and transportation. These, already fairly well organized, compose the bulk of the 16,000,000 members to whom President George Meany will be pointing with pride. Livingston, the husky auto worker from the Ozarks, will be concerned rather with the 45,000,000 wage earners outside the union fold. They include most women workers, most white-collar employees, and most of the men and women, white and Negro, employed in the South. If, within the next ten years he would double the membership of the A.F. of L.-C.I.O., his name would go down in labor history alongside that of John L. Lewis.

* "Organizing the Unorganized," *The Nation* CLXXXI (December 10, 1955), 497-500.

The car you now drive, the house you live in, the meat and bread you eat—these are all pretty likely to be union-made. Likewise the electrical gadgets you live by, your means of getting hither and yon, the structures you work in, the things you read are produced, chances are, by hands that hold a union card. It's not nearly so likely that the clothes you wear (unless you insist on the union label) will be union-made. Most of the food you eat, most of the personal services you receive, the host of small and inexpensive things—these are, by and large, without benefit of union protection to their makers, processors, and handlers.

The statistics which face Livingston in his organizing drive do not give the whole picture. For instance, Chicago. This cradle of American labor is less unionized, factory-wise, than Richmond, Virginia, or Birmingham, Alabama. Enormous segments of heavy industry, particularly in oil and chemicals, remain untouched by orthodox unionism. In certain industries where both A.F. of L. and C.I.O. have competing unions, as in meat packing, textiles, and chemicals, internecine strife has taken a heavy toll. But the key to Chicago's poor showing is the small factory. In this metropolitan area there are not fewer than 14,000 factories employing one million workers, and most of them have fewer than a thousand employees. Here unionism runs into cost factors and the law of diminishing returns. A union administrator will tell you that it costs only about twice as much to furnish union services in a plant with 1,000 members as in one with a hundred. The temptation here is to organize not the workers but the employers into associations to be more easily policed by association-wide contracts. Small factories are a major union problem almost everywhere; in the aggregate they may well account for 10,000,000 unorganized workers.

Another roadblock to unionism is the white-collar employee. The factory workers tend to be output minded and to tie this in with severely regimented wage scales, seniority and working rules. The office workers in the big industrial plants look with no little envy on the status production workers have attained; whether unions can modify their rigid notions to fit the white collar, while the white collar abandons some of his notions of superiority, will determine union success in this most promising of all the big unconquered sectors.

Women are a problem, too. Or rather, union men are the problem in their attitude toward organizing women. The traditional male idea has been that the husband, as family breadwinner, should earn enough to support his family. Unions helped mightily to get the children out of the factories, and some of them thought woman's place, too, was in the home. However desirable this old American dream may have been, the facts of life negate it. Women constitute one-third of the labor force; one-third of women over fourteen are at work. The new A.F. of L.-C.I.O. director of organization may know better than to try to stretch women on unionism's procrustean bed. Since he'll likely be too male-conscious to see the problem (not a single woman has ever been elected to the executive board of either labor federation), perhaps there should be a woman co-director of organization. That might rectify the present situation where men are averaging $3,469 in yearly earnings against $1,252 for women, who are actually 13 per cent worse off, wage-wise, than they were thirteen years ago. The catch phrase, so dear to both Republican and Democratic vote-catchers, that labor never had it so good, certainly doesn't apply to women.

Whatever his other problems, Director Livingston is not going to be bothered much by the size of his organizing budget. The new federation starts with a built-in annual deficit of between three and four million dollars. This stems from the facts of merger. Governed by sacrosanct rules of tenure and seniority, the merged federation will enjoy no economies but rather a two-headed bureaucracy in which every officeholder is assured of his job.

The lack of money doesn't mean too much. There were hardly pennies available back in the 1930's when steel, auto, electrical, and machine workers organized themselves. Sending scads of paid organizers into virgin territory usually doesn't pay off. The paid organizers are apt to limit their efforts to getting signatures on application cards; that indeed is the criterion of success in many a union headquarters. It is assumed that there is some magic in the word "union" and that this *deus ex machina* will do the job somehow by remote control. Wherever workers have been genuinely organized into unions, they have accepted the union as a vehicle which they must pull to success by their own efforts. It is true that there are many unions organized by bureaucratic methods, but they can better be described as workingmen's business organizations which come to life once a year when the contract expires. Unionism as a way of life, which is the biggest asset Director Livingston has in doubling the A.F. of L.-C.I.O. membership in the next decade, is a lot bigger than most union officials care to admit; in fact there is a certain tendency to lean over backwards and insist that the immediate pork chop is the sole goal of labor. A certain type of university intellectual who dabbles in labor matters fiercely loves this concept of business unionism, perhaps because it is supposed to be anti-Marxist, but few average citizens love it. It is a bit too materialistic to enlist widespread admiration among those not directly involved.

Business unionism will offer certain obstacles to Director Livingston's program. As these unions achieve a certain limited success, and their officials acquire financial and social status in rather sumptuous head-quarters, bureaucratism becomes a factor. So long as the dues continue to roll in, these cumbersome machines tend to rely on their own momentum to survive. While every union covets more per capita, the imagination and drive needed for organizing become dulled and the machines become involved in contemplating their own internal problems. Unable to cope with the challenge within their own industries, they look only with vague interest toward ambitious programs for organizing women, white collars, or the South. The typical union official today is an administrator, not an organizer. The situation was highlighted when the United Auto Workers offered to toss $1,250,000 into a general organizing kitty if other unions would also chip in. The idea lies vegetating in the fields and it will be interesting to see how much luck Director Livingston has in resurrecting it.

An exception must be noted. The Teamsters, an extremely self-centered and businesslike union, has garnered a rich harvest of small factories, warehouses, and processing plants. Almost any unorganized plant that a truck may enter to deliver or take away goods is subject to Teamsters' interest; so widespread has become its jurisdiction that it parallels in structure and scope the great British Transport and General Workers Union. While the Teamsters organize on a strictly self-centered basis which may afford little help to A.F. of L.-C.I.O.'s general campaigns, the success they have attained in aggressive organizing shows the possibilities lying around unrealized.

Another encouraging factor with which Director Livingston is well acquainted is the proletarianizing of the supervisory and technical staffs in heavy industry. In oil refineries, for example, there is now one supervisor for every five or six hourly workers. These, along with the technicians and professionals in the factory, are tending to become "the masses" and inclined to like the kind of protection that unionism affords.

This generation has seen two upsurges of organization, the first growing out of the desperation of the Great Depression, the second out of World War II. In the first, workers organized themselves. In the second, the unions did the job through labor-board ballots with a powerful assist from the government which needed to have war workers mobilized for more effective direction.

The current era differs from both. It can hardly be said that the unorganized show desperation today, particularly in the North. Many of them bask in the shade of the union umbrella without having to pay dues. Perhaps as many workers enjoy the wage benefits of unionism outside the unions as inside—they are the free riders. Then there are the millions of capitalism's captives, the indentured servants of installment purchases.

They feel they can't afford to risk strikes for the union because the sheriff might haul away the cherished TV, the beloved new car, or the housewife's proud badge of freedom, her machines for washing and cleaning. Not in their ranks of course are the appalling numbers even in the North who earn less than $1 an hour, but still are an influential minority among the unorganized.

Employers, too, have their umbrella, the Cadillac Cabinet in Washington, basically hostile to unionism. Lothair Teetor, former Assistant Secretary of Commerce whose Perfect Circle firm in Indiana believes in shooting it out with the United Auto Workers, hastily abandoned his Washington post not, perhaps, because his hostility to the union was repudiated but because this display of pre-Rooseveltian antiunionism was embarrassing. The Secretary of the Interior, whose struck Oregon firm depends more on starvation than bullets to beat down the union, rides more easily in the Cabinet. Under Eisenhower, the National Labor Relations Board has become a coolly hostile force from which unions can expect no favors. Insofar as possible, they bypass the very board which was set up originally to protect the right to organize. If a minor depression should set in, the unions, under the present Administration, might well find themselves entrenched in a war of self-preservation rather than in seeking more millions to organize.

Director Livingston then must face the intrinsic differences of this period, which contrasts with the 1930's and with the war years. There is an undeniable passivity among many unorganized workers and a growing intransigence among hard-boiled employers. These are high hurdles.

Any serious proposal to add millions to the labor movement must take into account the South, where industry is burgeoning, wages are low, and security generally nonexistent. The emancipation of Southern labor is the key not only to the creation of a truly national labor movement, but to the refreshment of American political life. A South brought up to national wage standards, liberated from industrial-plantation feudalists, and freed from bondage to the race issue would give a new turn to the national life. This long overdue emancipation can be labor's greatest gift both to the South and to the country at large. It will be achieved when Southern workers find the union key. They are ready, they are good joiners, and when they have pledged their work they are loyal to it (a mighty asset on the picket line). Here especially the spiritual values that labor can express find a ready response. Southern workers are tired of being second-class industrial citizens, of being told that sunshine is a good substitute for adequate pay and the self-respect that unions bring. Nor will the chains of installment-buying bind them; they have little to lose and much to win in a fight.

The textile baronies along the Atlantic Piedmont differ as sharply from the industrialized Birmingham region as does oil-rich Texas and the Southwest from either. There is no unified "South." Alongside the peonized sugar workers of Louisiana are unionized oil workers on the Gulf Coast who have wiped out the North-South wage differential. The Birmingham steel workers have just erased the wage differential; the meat packers are narrowing the margin. Along the bayous and in the piney woods giant new plants are mushrooming, most of them built by Northern corporations accustomed to dealing with unions up North. Any Southern organizer will tell you that a new plant is twice as easy (or half as difficult) to line up as an older one.

Nevertheless repeated "Southern drives" have petered out. A good bit of the blame must be placed at labor's door because of its hesitant attitude toward Negroes. A firm stand has been diluted out of concern for the prejudice of the white worker; as a result neither white nor Negro is organized.

There is no disguising the stubbornness of racial prejudice; on the other hand it has been magnified out of all perspective by the racist press and agitators. It is becoming increasingly clear to Southern workers that discrimination is holding back both races. All the way from Richmond to Corpus Christi union leaders can give concrete examples of success in fighting discrimination. The Negro, as an ally, can decide the issue of unionism in the South; if he is left uninterested, he can defeat unionism by his mere passivity. When the A.F. of L.-C.I.O brings its fight for economic and political equality out of the clouds of convention oratory and pious resolutions into a genuine fighting program, the next drive in the South will need neither millions of dollars nor thousands of paid organizers. To paraphrase Marx, the emancipation of the Southern workers will be achieved by the Southern workers themselves, once Negroes are assured a position in the labor movement fully equal to their white brothers.

The main reason organized labor has made little progress in recent years can be found in "public opinion." Director Livingston will find this public opinion the all-important factor in his organizing plans. Not the public opinion so readily manufactured by the mass media controlled by the business elements, but rather that of the grapevine, of word-of-mouth that spreads among unorganized workers as they eye unionism as it is. In this, the spiritual factors far outweigh the material, odd as that may seem. The name of John L. Lewis was magic to millions in the 1930's because at last one of their own stood up, fought back, and won against the titans of his time. That exhilaration of spirit was worth more than millions in the treasury. The image of Organized Labor as the protector of the poor, the apostle of public education, the champion of better health, and welfare, the watchdog against private plunder of the national resources, the advocate of world brotherhood, is the most valuable asset the A.F. of L.-C.I.O. director of organization can possibly have. That is why the business press has been so keen to show up sporadic pilfering of union welfare funds and to front-page the mansions of a few labor leaders. If the labor movement can be reduced in public estimation to a selfish materialistic concept in which a favored class advances its own pay (and prices to the public, as the press insists) and collaborates with municipal corruptionists for special privilege, the vast majority of men and women still outside the House of Labor will remain there. If labor's political action, in practice, seems aimed at seeking favors, in advancing the interests of political shysters, in urging expanding military expenditures so that unionized war workers in plane factories and other munitions plants may be sheltered, there will be little spark of response from the unorganized. Even if their aspirations are unverbalized, they seek security, dignity, peace.

In truth there have always been the two drives within the labor movement, the one animated by the highest concern for humanity, the other rather desperately seeking to find safety for some behind barriers. Across the country from coast to coast there are thousands dedicated to the proposition that unions are the engines of democracy in an industrial society; their voices are going to be heard increasingly as the bankruptcy in imagination and drive of the business unionists continues to breed sterility. It is to them that Director Livingston will need to be looking for the organizers, largely unpaid, of the millions who should be in the unified House of Labor.

"The Myth of the Happy Worker"—Harvey Swados (1957) *

"From where we sit in the company," says one of the best personnel men in the country, "we have to look at only the aspects of work that cut across all sorts of jobs—administration and human relations. Now these are aspects of work, abstractions, but it's easy for personnel people to get so hipped on their importance that they look on the specific tasks of making things and selling them as secondary . . ."
                        The Organization Man by William H. Whyte Jr.

The personnel man who made this remark to Mr. Whyte differed from his brothers only in that he had a moment of insight. Actually, "the spe-

* "The Myth of the Happy Worker," from *A Radical's America* by Harvey Swados (Boston: Atlantic Monthly Press, 1962). Copyright 1957 by Harvey Swados. First published in *Nation Magazine*, CLXXXV (August 17, 1957), 65-68. Reprinted by permission of the author and James Brown Associates, Inc.

cific tasks of making things" are now not only regarded by his white-collar fellows as "secondary," but as irrelevant to the vaguer but more "challenging" tasks of the man at the desk. This is true not just of the personnel man, who places workers, replaces them, displaces them—in brief, manipulates them. The union leader also, who represents workers and sometimes manipulates them, seems increasingly to regard what his workers do as merely subsidiary to the job he himself is doing in the larger community. This job may be building the Red Cross or the Community Chest, or it may sometimes be—as the Senate hearings suggest— participating in such communal endeavors as gambling, prostitution, and improving the breed. In any case, the impression is left that the problems of the workers in the background (or underground) have been stabilized, if not permanently solved.

With the personnel man and the union leader, both of whom presumably see the worker from day to day, growing so far away from him, it is hardly to be wondered at that the middle class in general, and articulate middle-class intellectuals in particular, see the worker vaguely, as through a cloud. One gets the impression that when they do consider him, they operate from one of two unspoken assumptions: (1) The worker has died out like the passenger pigeon, or is dying out, or becoming acculturated, like the Navajo; (2) If he is still around, he is just like the rest of us—fat, satisfied, smug, a little restless, but hardly distinguishable from his fellow TV viewers of the middle class.

Lest it be thought that (1) is somewhat exaggerated, I hasten to quote from a recently published article apparently dedicated to the laudable task of urging slothful middle-class intellectuals to wake up and live: "The old-style sweat-shop crippled mainly the working people. Now there are no workers left in America; we are almost all middle class as to income and expectations." I do not believe the writer meant to state— although he comes perilously close to it—that nobody works any more. If I understand him correctly, he is referring to the fact that the worker's rise in real income over the last decade, plus the diffusion of middle-class tastes and values throughout a large part of the underlying population, have made it increasingly difficult to tell blue-collar from white-collar worker without a program. In short, if the worker earns like the middle class, votes like the middle class, dresses like the middle class, dreams like the middle class, then he ceases to exist as a worker.

But there is one thing that the worker doesn't do like the middle class: he works like a worker. The steel mill puddler does not yet sort memos, the coal miner does not yet sit in conferences, the cotton mill hand does not yet sip martinis from his lunchbox. The worker's attitude toward his work is generally compounded of hatred, shame, and resignation.

Before I spell out what I think this means, I should like first to examine some of the implications of the widely held belief that "we are almost all middle class as to income and expectations." I am neither economist, sociologist, nor politician, and I hold in my hand no doctored statistics to be haggled over. I am by profession a writer who has had occasion to work in factories at various times during the Thirties, Forties, and Fifties. The following observations are simply impressions based on my last period of factory servitude, in 1956.

The average automobile worker gets a little better than two dollars an hour. As such he is one of the best-paid factory workers in the country. After twenty years of militant struggle led by the union that I believe to be still the finest and most democratic labor organization in the United States, he is earning less than the starting salaries offered to inexperienced and often semiliterate college graduates without dependents. After compulsory deductions for taxes, social security, old-age insurance and union dues, and optional deductions for hospitalization and assorted charities, his pay check for forty hours of work is going to be closer to seventy than to eighty dollars a week. Does this make him middle class as to income? Does it rate with the weekly take of a dentist, an accountant, a salesman, a draftsman, a journalist? Surely it would be more to the point to ask how a family man can get by in the Fifties on that kind of income. I know how he does it, and I should think the answers would be a little disconcerting to those who wax glib on the satisfactory status of the "formerly" underprivileged.

For one thing, he works a lot longer than forty hours a week—when he can. Since no automobile company is as yet in a position to guarantee its workers anything like fifty weeks of steady forty-hour paychecks, the auto worker knows he has to make it while he can. During peak production periods he therefore puts in nine, ten, eleven and often twelve hours a day on the assembly line for weeks on end. And that's not all. If he has dependents, as like as not, he also holds down a "spare time" job. I have worked on the line with men who doubled as mechanics, repairmen, salesmen, contractors, builders, farmers, cab drivers, lumberyard workers, countermen. I would guess that there are many more of these than show up in the official statistics: often a man will work for less if he can be paid under the counter with tax-free dollars.

Nor is that all. The factory worker with dependents cannot carry the debt load he now shoulders—the middle-class debt load, if you like, of nagging payments on car, washer, dryer, TV, clothing, house itself—without family help. Even if he puts in fifty, sixty or seventy hours a week at one or two jobs, he has to count on his wife's paycheck, or his son's, his daughter's, his brother-in-law's; or on his mother's social security, or his father's veteran's pension. The working-class family today is not typically held together by the male wage earner, but by multiple wage earners often of several generations who club together to get the things they want and need—or are pressured into believing they must have. It is at best a precarious arrangement; as for its toll on the physical organism and the psyche, that is a question perhaps worthy of further investigation by those who currently pronounce themselves bored with Utopia Unlimited in the Fat Fifties.

But what of the worker's middle-class expectations? I had been under the impression that this was the rock on which Socialist agitation had foundered for generations: it proved useless to tell the proletarian that he had a world to win when he was reasonably certain that with a few breaks he could have his own gas station. If these expectations have changed at all in recent years, they would seem to have narrowed rather than expanded, leaving a psychological increment of resignation rather than of unbounded optimism (except among the very young—and even among them the optimism focuses more often on better-paying opportunities elsewhere in the labor market than on illusory hopes of swift status advancement). The worker's expectations are for better pay, more humane working conditions, more job security. As long as he feels that he is going to achieve them through an extension of existing conditions, for that long he is going to continue to be a middle-class conservative in temper. But only for that long.

I suspect that what middle-class writers mean by the worker's middle-class expectations are his cravings for commodities—his determination to have not only fin-tailed cars and single-unit washer-dryers, but butterfly chairs in the rumpus room, African masks on the wall and power boats in the garage. Before the middle-class intellectuals condemn these expectations too harshly, let them consider, first, who has been utilizing every known technique of suasion and propaganda to convert luxuries into necessities, and second, at what cost these new necessities are acquired by the American working-class family.

Now I should like to return to the second image of the American worker: satisfied, doped by TV, essentially middle-class in outlook. This is an image bred not of communication with workers (except as mediated by fired interviewers sent "into the field" like anthropologists or entomologists), but of contempt for people, based perhaps on self-contempt and on a feeling among intellectuals that the worker has let them down. In order to see this clearly, we have to place it against the intellectual's changing attitudes toward the worker since the Thirties.

At the time of the organization of the C.I.O., the middle-class intellectual saw the proletarian as society's figure of virtue—heroic, magnanimous, bearing in his loins the seeds of a better future; he would have found ludicrous the suggestion that a sit-down striker might harbor anti-Semitic feelings. After Pearl Harbor, the glamorization of the worker was taken over as a function of government. Then, however, he was no longer the builder of the future good society; instead he was second only to the fighting man as the vital winner of the war. Many intellectuals, as government employees, found themselves helping to create this new portrait of the worker as patriot.

But in the decade following the war intellectuals have discovered that workers are no longer either building socialism or forging the tools of victory. All they are doing is making the things that other people buy. That, and participating in the great commodity scramble. The disillusionment, it would seem, is almost too terrible to bear. Word has gotten around among the highbrows that the worker is not heroic or idealistic; public opinion polls prove that he wants barbecue pits more than foreign aid and air conditioning more than desegregation, that he doesn't particularly want to go on strike, that he is reluctant to form a Labor Party, that he votes for Stevenson and often even for Eisenhower and Nixon—that he is, in short, animated by the same aspirations as drive the middle class onward and upward in suburbia.

There is of course a certain admixture of self-delusion in the middle-class attitude that workers are now the same as everybody else. For me it was expressed most precisely last year in the dismay and sympathy with which middle-class friends greeted the news that I had gone back to work in a factory. If workers are now full-fledged members of the middle class, why the dismay? What difference whether one sits in an office or stands in a shop? The answer is so obvious that one feels shame at laboring the point. But I have news for my friends among the intellectuals. The answer is obvious to workers, too.

They know that there is a difference between working with your back and working with your behind (I do not make the distinction between handwork and brainwork, since we are all learning that white-collar work is becoming less and less brainwork). They know that they work harder than the middle class for less money. Nor is it simply a question of status, that magic word so dear to the hearts of the sociologues, the new anatomizers of the American corpus. It is not simply status hunger that makes a man hate work which pays *less* than other work he knows about, if *more* than any other work he has been trained for (the only reason my fellow workers stayed in the assembly line, they told me again and again). It is not simply status hunger that makes a man hate work that is mindless, endless, stupefying, sweaty, filthy, noisy, exhausting, insecure in its prospects and practically without hope of advancement.

The plain truth is that factory work is degrading. It is degrading to any man who ever dreams of doing something worthwhile with his life; and it is about time we faced the fact. The more a man is exposed to middle-class values, the more sophisticated he becomes and the more production-line work is degrading to him. The immigrant who slaved in the poorly lighted, foul, vermin-ridden sweatshop found his work less degrading than the native-born high school graduate who reads Judge Parker, Rex Morgan, M.D., and Judd Saxon, Business Executive, in the funnies, and works in a fluorescent factory with ticker-tape production-control machines. For the immigrant laborer, even the one who did not dream of socialism, his long hours were going to buy him freedom. For the factory worker of the Fifties, his long hours are going to buy him commodities . . . and maybe reduce a few of his debts.

Almost without exception, the men with whom I worked on the assembly line last year felt like trapped animals. Depending on their age and personal circumstances, they were either resigned to their fate, furiously angry at *themselves* for what they were doing, or desperately hunting other work that would pay as well and in addition offer some variety, some prospect of change and betterment. They were sick of being pushed around by harried foremen (themselves more pitied than hated), sick of working like blinkered donkeys, sick of being dependent for their livelihood on a maniacal production-merchandising setup, sick of working in a place where there was no spot to relax during the twelve-minute rest period. (Some day—let us hope—we will marvel that production was still so worshipped in the Fifties that new factories could be built with every splendid facility for the storage and movement of essential parts, but with no place for a resting worker to sit down for a moment but on a fire plug, the edge of a packing case, or the sputum- and oil-stained stairway of a toilet.)

The older men stay put and wait for their vacations. But since the assembly line demands young blood (you will have a hard time getting hired if you are over thirty-five), the factory in which I worked was aswarm with new faces every day; labor turnover was so fantastic and absenteeism so rampant, with the young men knocking off a day or two every week to hunt up other jobs, that the company was forced to over-hire in order to have sufficient workers on hand at the starting siren.

To those who will object—fortified by their readings in C. Wright Mills and A. C. Spectorsky—that the white-collar commuter, too, dislikes his work, accepts it only because it buys his family commodities, and is constantly on the prowl for other work, I can only reply that for me at any rate this is proof not of the disappearance of the working class but of the proletarianization of the middle class. Perhaps it is not taking place quite in the way that Marx envisaged it, but alienation of the white-collar man (like that of the laborer) from both his tools and whatever he produces, the slavery that chains the exurbanite to the commuting timetable (as the worker is still chained to the timeclock), the anxiety that sends the white-collar man home with his briefcase for an evening's work (as it degrades the workingman into pleading for long hours of overtime), the displacement of the white-collar slum from the wrong side of the tracks to the suburbs (just as the working-class slum is moved from old-law tenements to skyscraper barracks)—all these mean to me that the white-collar man is entering (though his arms may be loaded with commodities) the gray world of the working man.

Three quotations from men with whom I worked may help to bring my view into focus:

Before starting work: "Come on, suckers, they say the Foundation wants to give away *more* than half a billion this year. Let's do and die for the old Foundation."

During rest period: "Ever stop to think how we crawl here bumper to bumper, and crawl home bumper to bumper, and we've got to turn out more every minute to keep our jobs, when there isn't even any room for them on the highways?"

At quitting time (this from older foremen, whose job is not only to keep things moving, but by extension to serve as company spokesmen): "You're smart to get out of here. . . . I curse the day I ever started, now I'm stuck: any man with brains that stays here ought to have his head examined. This is no place for an intelligent human being."

Such is the attitude toward the work. And toward the product? On the one hand it is admired and desired as a symbol of freedom, almost a substitute for freedom, not because the worker participated in making it, but because our whole culture is dedicated to the proposition that the automobile is both necessary and beautiful. On the other hand it is hated and despised—so much that if your new car smells bad it may be due to a banana peel crammed down its gullet and sealed up thereafter, so much so that if your dealer can't locate the rattle in your new car you might ask him to open the welds on one of those tail fins and vacuum out the nuts and bolts thrown in by workers sabotaging their own product.

Sooner or later, if we want a decent society—by which I do not mean a society glutted with commodities or one maintained in precarious equilibrium by overbuying and forced premature obsolescence—we are going to have to come face to face with the problem of work. Apparently the Russians have committed themselves to the replenishment of their labor force through automatic recruitment of those intellectually incapable of keeping up with severe scholastic requirements in the public educational system. Apparently we, too, are heading in the same direction: although our economy is not directed, and although college education is as yet far from free, we seem to be operating in this capitalist economy on the totalitarian assumption that we can funnel the underprivileged, undereducated, or just plain underequipped, into the factory, where we can proceed to forget about them once we have posted the minimum fair labor standards on the factory wall.

If this is what we want, let's be honest enough to say so. If we conclude that there is nothing noble about repetitive work, but that it is nevertheless good enough for the lower orders, let's say that, too, so we will at least know where we stand. But if we cling to the belief that other men are our brothers, not just Egyptians, or Israelis, or Hungarians, but *all* men, including millions of Americans who grind their lives away on an insane treadmill, then we will have to start thinking about how their work and their lives can be made meaningful. That is what I assume the Hungarians, both workers and intellectuals, have been thinking about. Since no one has been ordering us what to think, since no one has been forbidding our intellectuals to fraternize with our workers, shouldn't it be a little easier for us to admit, first, that our problems exist, then to state them, and then to see if we can resolve them?